Advance Praise for Elaine Clayton's

Making Marks

"In her book, Elaine Clayton knows how to blend her huge artistic talent with our inner consciousness and genetic spiritual nature, resulting in the positive emotional rewards we all seek."

—**James D. Baird, PhD**, author of the award-winning *Happiness Genes*

"With her wise insights, engaging sketches, and easy-to-follow exercises, Elaine Clayton has made me a convert of 'stream drawing,' or intuitive drawing. *Making Marks* is a magical toolkit for exploring our deeper, instinctual selves that I recommend to anyone wanting to live life more richly and joyfully."

—**Mary Reynolds Thompson**, author of *Embrace Your Inner Wild* and *Reclaiming the Wild Soul*

"As a dream expert who dabbles in art, I love this book! Its deep and delightful insights evoke the glee of a child sliding down a banister as you ride into a greater awareness of yourself and the ties that bind your creativity and intuition. This book connects you to your soul."

—**Stase Michaels**, author of *The Bedside Guide to Dreams* and *Two-Minute Dream Techniques*

"In *Making Marks*, Elaine Clayton presents a creative and enlightening way to engage your whole being in self-discovery by drawing on the intuitive language of your soul. Clear pencil-and-paper exercises gently engage the whole brain and physical senses to provide a treasury of insights toward a deeper relationship with self and others. It is an engaging, enlightening, and enjoyable journey from beginning to end!"

—**Aila Accad, RN, MSN**, author of *The Call of The Soul*

"The benefit of art practice is not limited to producing a work of art. It is a way of finding the space between rational thinking and intuitive discovery. This wonderful book is a guide to help everyone locate and explore the space in-between."

—**Marshall Arisman**, world-renowned painter, illustrator, educator

"Ancient drawings on rocks, in caves, on bones. Black Elk's *Tree of Life*. A Lakota winter count. These images moved across my mind as I read *Making Marks*. Ever since I can remember, they have triggered my imaginings, caused me to wonder about the nature of life and death, and even tapped my awakening spirit. Simple and yet deeply complex, primordial drawings tell us something about the way our ancestors saw themselves, and the world in which they lived, at a time we otherwise could not know. Artist, teacher, and author, Elaine Clayton returns us to a sense of that kind of expression we so desperately need in this so technologically driven society. . . . [She] can be our ethnographer, our docent, and even our curator in this remarkably simple, artistic exploration and interpretation of ourselves."

—**Gabriel Horn**, author of *Transcendence* and *The Book of Ceremonies*

"Elaine Clayton shows us how the value of drawing for pure pleasure can transform our lives. Clayton demonstrates how drawing can connect us to our deeper senses, allowing us to make wise decisions. In this fast-paced world, we need tools that help us slow down and reflect. In *Making Marks*, Clatyon shares the tools that provide an effective means to gain new insights and make important life decisions."

—**Marga Odahowski**, director of studies for the International Residential College, University of Virginia and author of *The Way of the Hammock*

"Elaine Clayton reminds us all that the simple act of mark making can be a generative act. She unpacks the contemporary mental constructs that obscure the power of drawing first discovered by our earliest human ancestors, and invites us through this primal activity to dive back into the well of the possible."

—**Maria Artemis**, internationally known sculptor

"A wonderful vacation from everyday life and mind awaits you in this book. Set the lines free and see where you go!"

—**Karen Rauch Carter**, author and joyfully-drawing book signer of *Make a Shift, Change Your Life*

"Drawing is a powerful act that can tap into a deep-seated, intuitive process involved with creativity and the emotional life. Elaine Clayton's *Making Marks* facilitates intuition, releasing the mind to discover new ideas, creative inspiration, and unexpected solutions."

—**Dr. Raymond Moody, MD, PhD**

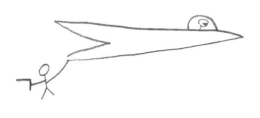

"This is a remarkable book. It shows how a universal urge to make marks can be a doorway to dimensions of consciousness of which we're unaware in our waking life. This book is Big Majick, revealing how something utterly ordinary can become sacred and transcendent. Want to unleash your inner Picasso or Paul Klee? Read Clayton's captivating book!"

—**Larry Dossey, MD**, author of
One Mind and *The Science of Premonitions*

"When you pick up a pencil and allow yourself the freedom to make marks and lines, your hand can unlock deeply held memories and emotions that are beyond words. In *Making Marks*, Elaine Clayton describes her original process for awakening the reader's creative, intuitive awareness. Whether or not you think you have artistic talent, this book will give you the self-confidence to explore your own hidden potentials."

—**Laurie Nadel, PhD**,
bestselling author of *Sixth Sense*

Making Marks

DISCOVER THE ART OF INTUITIVE DRAWING

ELAINE CLAYTON

ATRIA PAPERBACK
New York London Toronto Sydney New Delhi

BEYOND WORDS
Hillsboro, Oregon

ATRIA PAPERBACK
A Division of Simon & Schuster, Inc.
1230 Avenue of the Americas
New York, NY 10020

BEYOND WORDS
20827 N.W. Cornell Road, Suite 500
Hillsboro, OR 97124-9808
503-531-8700 / 503-531-8773 fax
www.beyondword.com

Managing editor: Lindsay S. Brown
Editors: Sheila Ashdown, Anna Noak
Copyeditor: Claire Rudy Foster
Proofreader: Michelle Blair
Interior Design: Devon Smith
Composition: William H. Brunson Typography Services

First Atria Paperback/Beyond Words trade paperback edition May 2014

ATRIA PAPERBACK and colophon are trademarks of Simon & Schuster, Inc.

Beyond Words Publishing is an imprint of Simon & Schuster, Inc. and the Beyond Words logo is a registered trademark of Beyond Words Publishing, Inc.

For more information about special discounts for bulk purchases, please contact Simon & Schuster Special Sales at 1-866-506-1949 or business@simonandschuster.com.

The Simon & Schuster Speakers Bureau can bring authors to your live event. For more information or to book an event, contact the Simon & Schuster Speakers Bureau at 1-866-248-3049 or visit our website at www.simonspeakers.com.

Manufactured in the United States of America

10 9 8 7 6 5 4 3 2 1

Library of Congress Cataloging-in-Publication Data:

Clayton, Elaine.
    Making marks : discover the art of intuitive drawing / Elaine Clayton.—First Atria Paperback/Beyond Words trade paperback edition.
        pages   cm
    Includes index.
    1. Drawing, Psychology of.   2. Creation (Literary, artistic, etc.)—Psychological aspects.   3. Intuition.   I. Title.
    BF456.D7C53 2014
    741.01'9—dc23

                                                                                    2013045469

ISBN 978-1-58270-422-7
ISBN 978-1-4767-1309-0 (ebook)

The corporate mission of Beyond Words Publishing, Inc.: *Inspire to Integrity*

This book is dedicated to Kenneth Clayton, MSAT, BFA,
whose contributions, loving guidance, and deeply informing,
empathic knowledge helped this book come into being.

Thanks to all who have made their
own marks and contributed
wonderful drawings to this book.

Contents

Foreword by Eldon Taylor   xiii

Preface   xv

Introduction: Discovering Your Intuitive Self through the Power of Drawing   xxi

1. Reframing: A New Way to Look at Drawing   1

2. Stream Drawing: Getting into the Flow   11

3. Playing with Your Perception of Line   21

4. Drawing on the Past: Memory Drawing   51

5. Drawing Out Emotion: Empathic Curiosity and Imaginative Interplay   71

6. Streaming and Dreaming: The Link between Dreams and Intuition   83

7. Visionary: How to Read a Stream Drawing   103

8. Seeing Is Believing: Intuitive Stream Drawing Readings   113

9. Streaming for Answers: Gaining Insight into Life's Questions   127

10. Celebrating the Lives of Others through Stream Drawing   135

11. Drawing as a Pathway to Intuitive Discoveries at Home and Abroad   159

Acknowledgments   173

Index of Exercises   175

Index of Figures   177

A Quick Look at Visual-Intuitive Meanings   181

Foreword

Elaine Clayton has a rare gift that she has chosen to share with you. Imagine opening up to a yet-uncharted region of yourself and discovering with great excitement an entirely new dimension of your being. What Elaine offers is somewhat akin to giving sight to the blind or hearing to the deaf. Indeed, it is a genuine, added sensory lens that leads to understanding new richness and depth in many of our experiences.

If you knew that visual imagery offered intuitive knowledge, would you begin to see differently? What if you were able to create imagery that provided insight into life's questions? In *Making Marks*, Elaine Clayton shares her explorations in intuitive discovery through drawing and seeks to encourage others in using the same method she developed over a lifetime of creating images. With Elaine's guidance, you will discover new meaning, potential, and even purpose where you may have never seen it before.

Making Marks supports seeing intuitively through stream-of-consciousness drawing, a skill that empowers the seer just as listening to the "quiet voice within" empowers the listener to be guided toward truth. In our capitalist society, we use visual imagery to buy and sell without understanding the profound impact that imagery has on us. Through the simple act of making marks, portals to knowing open before us. This book shows us how to make and create marks that will enlighten and delight us. Learning to see and sense the "personality" in the simplest mark will help us become aware of the subtle but powerful influence images have on us; our responses guide us to a better understanding of our place in the world. This deeper awareness empowers us to respond consciously, make better choices for happiness and well-being, and open our hearts and minds so that we may create the life we wish to live.

I have had the pleasure to work with Elaine and to witness firsthand the skill she shares in *Making Marks*. I have often paraphrased an old Sufi saying like this: "The value of a book is not in what it says, but rather in what it *does*." This book will provide you with a new skill set that will reveal your life in a new light, empowering you to *do* what's necessary to realize your highest self.

—Eldon Taylor

Preface

From the time I could hold a pencil, crayon, or marker, I made marks on anything I could find. Luckily, I was given a special wall to draw on, and nobody ever chastised me for drawing on the pristine white endpapers of books!

I mostly drew people. My curiosity about people was strong early on, and has only increased over time. That curiosity had an invisible momentum for me, as I sensed the underlying force within people, expressed in their physical features, their choice of clothing, and other attributes that highlighted the ways in which they were the same or similar to me, and the ways in which they were different. I drew as a response to that momentum, this mystery about who we are as people—and people arrived for me on paper. I re-created them, whether it was a composite of people I had met or seen, or a portrait. I would inwardly listen to them as they came into being—they told me their names ("Buddy-Randy" was one young boy, see Figure 1) and showed me their clothes and let me in on their lives, their likes and dislikes, and their stories. They were so very real to me that I remember a harrowing feeling when I erased one of these drawn people one day—I understood that I could never get that exact person back. It was as if I had a real person there on paper in front of me; with a few strokes of my eraser, she was gone forever. I could try to redraw her,

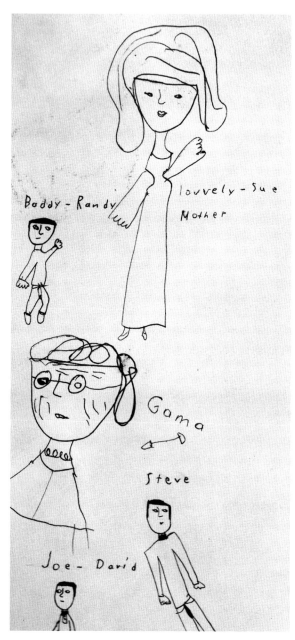

Figure 1.
My drawing of Buddy-Randy and his
family on a book's endpapers.

but that original version of her, accompanied by the "realness" of her being, could never be brought back in the same way. I think that moment helped me comprehend mortality in a deeper way than I had before. I was the one who created her, and I was the one who erased her. It felt like more than just a "nothing" thing—it felt very real to me. I sensed a kind of gravity around creating people on paper. I felt the power of my creative will, blended with a sense of vulnerability. The empowering feeling of drawing and making decisions around it took on a different tone from that point on. Making marks became my way of finding meaning and grasping life and death. I was going inward, nurturing my imaginative and creative urge to understand the world. I was expressing my curiosity and understanding by making meaningful marks.

"Going inward" had another meaning for me as well. My childhood was filled with stories of paranormal phenomena—starting with my own birth. My mother, as I was told, was near death at my birth and had experienced what is known today as a "near death experience," or NDE. While doctors tried to revive her, she became aware of herself floating above the operating table. She felt very ill at ease out of her body. She witnessed her other children waiting in a car with a babysitter outside the hospital and desperately wanted to remain with them. Luckily for us all, she survived the birth trauma. I heard the story recounted a few times, including the part where my Grandmother Clayton said that I was born "with a veil" over my face, signifying the gift of clairvoyance. I believe she was referring to the sac covering my face as I was lifted out during my mother's emergency C-section. (This means that there must be thousands of psychics out there, since C-sections are more common today). This family story, and many others about psychic phenomena—such as family members who had visions and premonitions—were part of my childhood identity. I heard them right along with fairy tales, poems, and stories about angels and saints.

Hearing these accounts nurtured my sense of wonder and curiosity about life and the unseen or spiritual nature of life. It gave me a longing to know the mysteries and forces that animate our lives, and a sense that there is more to our experience than what seems obvious. It was the same feeling I had while studying and drawing people: momentum, an unseen quality that gives life meaning. I felt moved by the spirit within and grew to appreciate the capacity we all have to know more than just what is on the surface. The experience of drawing people while feeling stirred by these mysteries remains with me.

I continued to draw and develop intuitively through adolescence. My drawings were mostly personal, though some professional jobs came my way; I was hired to paint signs and create scenes for framed art, cards, portraits, and T-shirt designs. By the time I was in high school, I was keeping dream journals. I had highly cinematic and emotional dreams each night and often woke up feeling overwhelmed by the images and emotional weight they held for me. At the time, my heroes were NDE pioneer researcher Raymond Moody, Edgar Cayce, and spiritual psychologist Carl Jung. I was also learning a great deal from my holistic physician dad, a D.O. who was certified and taught self-hypnosis techniques as early as the 1950s to help pregnant women have pain-free deliveries. My dad's compassion and natural desire to heal others grew as he grew; by the time I was middle-school age, he made a switch into psychiatry when that field was still focused on talk-analysis as the focus of healing. His quest to learn more was one of the greatest motivators for me in my search to understand myself in relation to healing, creativity, and intuition. Throughout my teen years I relied on him for guidance with the many questions I had about dreams and the human psyche.

My quest for deep knowledge of both art and intuition continued during college and into my adult life. I earned degrees in drawing and painting and in visual essay. I worked at a museum and taught children as an artist-in-residence in schools. This helped me form a philosophy about the purpose of art and empathic sensing. While teaching in progressive, independent schools in Atlanta and Boston, I was free to experiment in a thoroughly positive environment. During those years, I developed an empathic drawing workshop. The technique was created to help children enjoy making marks together in a noncompetitive and emotionally supportive atmosphere. I realized that children and adults responded enthusiastically to having a chance to draw while opening their hearts toward others. I have taken this workshop to libraries, museums, and schools throughout America. I have seen exciting shifts in both children and adults, as they go from apprehension to joy at the easel. I've witnessed empathy, cooperation, and creativity—large groups of individuals cultivating their own sense of compassion through drawing together. In my teaching, I use drawing every day as a method of discovery. I have written and illustrated several picture books, feeling inspired by what children taught me.

At the same time, I began to develop my intuition by using many different methods, such as tea leaf reading, psychometry, dream interpretation, vision quests, and palm reading. Sometimes the intuitive explorations were for fun, and other times for seeking answers to serious questions. Over time, I did intuitive readings for strangers. What started as spontaneous interactions at restaurants, parties, or other gatherings eventually developed into a professional practice. I devoted my studio time more and more to combined intuitive reading and art; gradually, I saw that intuition and drawing are connected in significant ways. Drawing is a vehicle toward intuitive opening and sensing. It provides a pathway into deeper feeling and thinking.

In time, I started creating drawings for the specific purpose of accessing intuitive information. Creating a drawing on behalf of another, what I call an "intuitive stream drawing reading," is a method of using stream-of-consciousness drawing as an intuitive guide. I have found that this method is remarkably beneficial. I knew I had to develop this technique and share it with others. I celebrate the chance to do just that, and I celebrate the merging of my two favorite subjects: drawing and intuition.

The creation of my first book on intuition, *Illuminara Intuitive Journal with Cards*, was the beginning. With this book, I shared how to intentionally use visual imagery to unlock the creative, imaginative, and intuitive spirit within. *Making Marks* takes that one step further. *Making Marks* is all about using visual imagery, but it uses drawing as part of the process of gathering intuitive knowledge in honor of the self. What I've discovered is that the answers we seek are not hidden, nor are they residing in someone else who is wiser or more skilled than we are. We each have our own unlimited potential to listen inward and be guided by that mysterious wellspring of knowledge and understanding. We all have the creative forces of life and free will, which animate us and inform our choices. Through drawing, we can activate the intention to heal and better understand ourselves within our world.

I hope this book will reflect my love of mark making and using drawing for personal, intuitive searching. I hope to help you discover and reach new levels of consciousness. You can delve deeper into your own core of being, as well as the aspect within you that can help heal others. Through making marks, we bring what is outside in. We make marks to bring what is inside out—emerging stronger and more aware of our purpose, creative power, and innate ability to empathize and bond with those around us.

—Elaine Clayton, MFA, BFA, Reiki Master

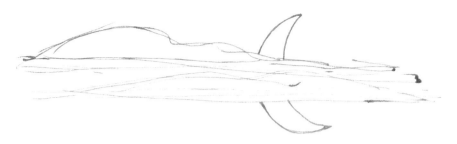

Introduction: Discovering Your Intuitive Self through the Power of Drawing

Have you ever had an inkling, hunch, or gut feeling? What did you do with it? Did you ignore it, or did you listen to that quiet voice inside—and feel glad that you did? Your intuitive intelligence is the quiet knowing that guides and informs you. The inner voice prompts you toward your best choices in life. But we often ignore that voice, or never even know it is there. *Making Marks* is an interactive book created to show you how to access the intuitive wellspring within you. Using drawing, you can enhance your life in every way. Stream-of-consciousness drawing, or "stream drawing," will open your senses as you develop the skills to become aligned with your intuitive and empathic sensing.

Making Marks is about discovering your intuitive self through the power of drawing. It is about getting into creative, imaginative flow and intuitive sensing through drawing from the heart, with innovative and playful techniques. You'll explore a treasure trove of ideas, solutions to problems, and answers to questions through tapping into the unconscious by drawing. Drawing intuitively opens the stream-of-consciousness, unlocking the mind and spirit to a future of dreams come true, healing the past, and giving assurance in each present moment. Through drawing, a natural and innate human urge, readers will increase empathic, intuitive sensing and be amazed at how easy it is to follow those inklings toward a life rich in love, abundance, and joy.

Reclaiming Our Right as Mark Makers

Making Marks puts a powerful empathic tool back where it belongs: in your hands. Drawing is an intuitive, rewarding, and essential part of self-discovery. Drawing is a link between our most internal, indwelling state of being, and the world around us. Drawing is the act of responding to the world and asking the world to acknowledge us (and our unique take on the world). Yet for many adults, the act of drawing has lost its meaning. To reclaim mark making, we must understand how we lost the urge to draw and rediscover its true benefits.

Our lives are meant to be full of abundance and joy, yet in order to experience true happiness, we need to know who we are. In order to find the answers we seek, we need to know our own questions. Drawing can support you as you re-create your life. With so many benefits, it's hard to understand why adults don't draw the way they used to when they were young. How did such a natural, positive, and empowering way of expressing the human spirit get squeezed out? I believe that this change happens gradually for most people.

From early childhood, the very young draw with true glee. There is something intrinsically rewarding and compelling about making marks and changing how a surface looks. Babies delight in swishing food around on their high-chair tray. They use all ten fingers to expand their creations, moving their arms and hands in circular motions. As a baby grows, drawing remains part of self-discovery. Many parents describe the look of pride on their toddler's face after she has scrawled on the walls. She says, "Look what I made!"

Young people simply follow the natural impulse to draw. It feels good to interact with our surroundings using the simplest gestures. It's as if we were saying, "Recognize me." In our young hearts, we know that we are individuals with the ability to alter our environment, and we get excited about it. We have free will to effect change! We've always known that drawing is proof of individual determination, our unique ability to make a difference in the world. Making marks activates our human desire to create, drawing on our emotions and experiences.

However, as we grow up and enter school, we lose our innocence and are no longer unconscious mark makers. We become part of a larger group with culturally conditioned, specific expectations. Since we spend most of our waking hours in school during childhood, that experience plays an enormous role in how we develop. It also influences what we feel about ourselves as well as what or who we perceive ourselves to be as adults.

In school, the meaning of making marks shifts. We begin making marks for approval. The alphabet and numbers are first and foremost—linear expressions. Learning to write means developing a disciplined way of making marks, which replaces the feeling of free expression in drawing. Although we first begin to draw when asked to try writing in school, we learn quickly that we can no longer make marks only for pleasure. The pressure to perform and be "correct" enters our psyche.

It is easy to conclude that drawing for fun, expression, and creative thrill became sidelined by other worthy work. Many veer away from drawing altogether, as the natural good feelings it brought slip into the shadows. The inner natural mark maker got repressed in one way or another. But I believe that the lively interplay between thought and emotion can be recaptured at any age.

This book will show that drawing has a serious, constructive place in our lives. It can aid us throughout life, from early childhood straight through to old age. This book will take you on an expedition with drawing that will reveal your personal, intuitive creative process. Stream drawing can calm the nerves and open the mind and heart to new self-acceptance. Stress turns to "just being" and feeling good. We open up to new ideas, pay attention to our emotions, and become more consciously aware of our surroundings. We begin to feel that we are part of our environment: much of what we feel *inside* can be seen symbolically *outside* in the world around us. Drawing lets us celebrate our inner knowing and helps us feel whole in our daily life, family, and community.

Making Marks will show you the benefits of stream drawing and teach you how to connect to a deeper sense of self and your environment. Stream drawing takes you from feeling separate and removed from everything (and feeling compartmen-talized) to a sense of oneness. You'll learn to take notice of the synchronistic events and intriguing signs that pull all the elements of life together. Your new awareness will make the days brighter. Discovering synchronistic events in ordinary daily life can inspire you to imagine how things could have happened, and why. Asking why is a way to engage in the world prior to making your own marks in it.

You may discover that this book prompts you to ask more questions or to imagine new approaches to problem solving: What if we all took time to draw for about ten minutes each day? If we were able to center our thoughts and feelings through drawing, and encourage others to do so, would we feel different? What if we used drawing to help us process feelings we could not describe verbally, or to aid children in improving core subjects such as math, literature, or science? What if we used drawing to connect with our ideals and wishes? And what if we were taught to state an intention of our choice before drawing to music at the start of our day? Follow your intuition and keep drawing as you move deeper into the stream of awareness and your new consciousness. Your new creative practice will bring you the answers you're looking for.

What Will You Gain from Reading This Book?

Making Marks will show you what you forgot you knew. It will put back into your hands the tool that is rightfully yours. You can recapture the spirit of excitement at making marks purely, from a natural impulse. This book will also teach you how to examine your marks to gain insight, often in unexpected ways!

This book teaches the safe and non-goal-oriented technique called stream draw-ing, which gives access to the immense power of intuitive healing. Stream drawing has two functions. One is to learn how to get into a creative flow by doing stream drawings; the other is to do stream drawings for the purpose of conducting intuitive readings. I will guide you through a step-by-step method of making stream draw-ings. Once you know how to tap into your flow, I will teach you how to do intuitive stream drawing readings. You'll learn how to use drawing to access your personal

unconscious memory and to increase and develop your intuitive intelligence. With practice, you will have literally at your fingertips a technique that will help you to intuit, see, and find solutions for yourself and others through drawing. You'll be able to develop your own visual, intuitive language.

In your discovery process, you will draw with an open mind and heart toward empathic, intuitive sensing. Your mind and heart are your essence—your "home"—and they possess more dimensions than you realize. You will discover there are rooms in your house that you never knew you had! The journey will require you to step out and go with the flow toward deeper inner knowing. Bit by bit, you will build an empathic, artistic, and robust visionary skill.

In Chapter 1, you'll have a chance to think of drawing in a new light and redis-cover something that is inherently yours. In Chapter 2, you'll get into the flow of stream-of-consciousness drawing with a feeling of freedom and expression, bridg-ing the gap between your unconscious and conscious mind and opening your heart to deeper awareness. In Chapter 3, you'll play with your perception of line and begin developing a way of seeing and sensing character and intuitive information. Once you've established the foundations of stream drawing, Chapters 4 and 5 will teach you to use these techniques to draw on memories and emotions, unlock the unconscious, and increase intuitive knowing. In Chapter 6, we'll explore the link between dreams and intuition: you'll develop empowerment through dreams, and move toward deeper intuitive knowledge. In Chapters 7 and 8, you'll explore the innate meanings of stream drawings. Then, in Chapters 9 and 10, you'll see how to use stream drawings with empathy and compassion to help yourself and others find guidance. Finally, in Chapter 11, we'll explore ways to use stream drawing to connect with your self and the world around you, at home, work, and in your community.

A List of What You Will Need

First, let me say that you do not have to buy any new drawing supplies. You may already have tons of scrap paper. This will work just fine if the sheets are at least eight-by-ten inches and blank on at least one side. You probably have pencils or pens that you can use. If you feel that getting new supplies would be exciting and fun and not too expensive, then go ahead. The point is to stay very uninhibited with your tools and be free to use them with abandon! If new supplies lock you up and you feel you'd be too careful or uptight about new "special" art paper, charcoal, or art pencils, then don't get the supplies yet. I suggest you use scrap paper at first and wait until you have the feeling of flow, freedom, and looseness you need in order to really draw with zeal—then you can splurge on new supplies. Remember that there is no wrong or right way; the supplies are there to support you. They are for you to use with joy and a sense of satisfaction.

Paper—Newsprint pad or large white drawing pad (eight-by-ten inches or larger).

Pencils—Art pencils. B3 and B6 are my favorites, but any pencil you feel comfortable using is fine.

Charcoal—Vine charcoal. It wipes away easily so you can use the same piece of paper over and over for your drawing explorations.

Sketchbook—As you progress with this book, you may want to practice in a large, blank sketchbook (eight-by-ten inches or larger).

In the final analysis, a drawing simply is no longer a drawing, no matter how self-sufficient its execution may be. It is a symbol, and the more profoundly the imaginary lines of projection meet higher dimensions, the better.

—**Paul Klee**

Reframing: A New Way to Look at Drawing

Drawing is a pathway to unconscious knowledge. There are two fundamental ways drawing functions as a catalyst for accessing deeper self-knowledge: first in the creation of a drawing, and then in reflecting on the creation. Drawing (and how we think and feel about it) has to do with perception. To draw is to feel, to emote, to express thought and feeling through line, shape, texture, and color. Comprehending or perceiving what has been drawn means finding meaning through thought, emotion, memory, and association. We perceive uniquely based upon our response to our environment and experiences, and that uniqueness is our own world of knowledge. Drawing engages cognition, the logical mind, while also waking our senses and inviting our emotions and thoughts to flow. Our conscious mind begins to work in unison with our unconscious mind. Making marks in a relaxed, meditative state allows the brain to function in harmony, opening us up to our full potential. Drawing fearlessly, with a sense of playfulness and pleasure in expression, widens the possibility for us to think and to feel harmoniously as both hemispheres become fully activated. Unconscious or unknown truths come into our awareness as ideas, solutions, and realizations. Through drawing, we realize what ideas or beliefs we were not aware of having. The conscious and unconscious—logic and intuition—are linked by the act of drawing.

For this to happen, you must make marks without "self-editing." Try to draw without hovering over yourself, directing, or criticizing yourself before you even get into a spontaneous, creative flow. You may have experienced this kind of loose, freestyle drawing when you were a young child, or perhaps more recently in an art class or on your own. Most likely you have drawn on the margins of paper, enjoying the marks you were making, commonly referred to as a "doodle." And part of the reason you enjoyed these "doodles" is because you were relaxed about it; the marks you made were only for fun, or to help you endure a long, boring lecture at school or a meeting at work. Maybe you were doodling because you were nervous or anxious; spinning out what seemed like little insignificant drawings made you feel calmer inside. However, this kind of so-called insignificant drawing is *tremendously* significant. Even the smallest mark has a universe of information in it. The process you engaged in while doing these little drawings is incredibly powerful. By making marks with a relaxed or self-soothing disposition, you entered into a special relationship to yourself. You opened the floodgates to your imagination, your infinite potential to create.

Something happens when a mark is made, and this is where the gold is. You can change an open surface or blank piece of paper. Your choice to create a mark where there was nothing before has power; that force in and of itself is symbolic of life, human experience, and free will.

Let's Change the Language!: No Such Thing as a "Doodle"

Many people in my workshops have described hearing derogatory comments about their drawings—some bad enough to make them stop drawing altogether. Even well-meaning remarks can sting. Comments vary from things like "What a silly doodle!" or "That drawing is not very good" to even worse, "That's a bad drawing; it doesn't even look like anything." Somebody may ask a child, "When are you going to stop fooling around and get serious?" implying that making art is a diversion, an irresponsible choice compared to more "respectable" ways to spend time and energy. The criticism people have about drawing is based on whether or not the viewer perceives the artist to have correctly captured his subject. It may also indicate a basic lack of appreciation for time spent making art.

Hearing these judgments is a natural result of growing up in a busy world that is becoming more technical each day and less focused on "old fashioned" art forms. Compared with fast-paced computer technology, drawing may not seem significant or useful. Teachers and parents try to raise children to be good self-advocates and help them develop the skills that will best prepare them for adult life. Believing that students are best served when they are educated with an emphasis on technology, science, and math, school culture veers heavily in that direction. Technology so rapidly advances and changes that it is indeed essential that time and resources be given to it to prepare and allow children to participate and innovate in a technological world. However, this means that when a school budget is cut, art is often the first thing to go, while technology-related classes and resources are given a priority. Making art is not as urgent as keeping up with technology. This choice seems to tell young people that drawing is not important—which isn't true at all. Drawing does not *take away* from learning other skills: in fact, it can enhance a person's sense of self. Drawing provides an opening for the artist to relax, quietly focus, elevate mental focus, and cultivate the mind more fully. It is a natural way of entering into a state of calm where we can bring forth our imagination and intuitive sensing and thinking skills. Drawing alleviates tension and also gives us the kind of bliss that arrives with other forms of meditation.

Calling a drawing a "doodle" conveys a very big message: a doodle is not a drawing and it is not important. We might as well call drawings "thingamajigs." Long ago I stopped using the word "doodle" while I was teaching. That word simply did not reflect the respect and enthusiasm I had for my students' work. I think we should change the language. I like to use the term "stream drawing" (and, in this book, "intuitive stream drawing readings") instead. To me, what people call "doodles" are wonderful drawings, and they deserve a name that honors what is special and significant in them.

I give full credit to my math coach/artist friends Connie Henry and Polly Wagner, who helped me align with a word that I felt had more integrity than the term "doodle." One day, I explained to them what I was doing with stream-of-consciousness drawing. I said that sometimes I felt like drawing was not respected or understood in our culture, and described the condescension I heard around the topic of drawing, giving me the impression that even very formally educated people may not understand the value in drawing. I explained that the lack of respect for it as an intelligent practice devalued and diminished artists and discouraged many more people from trying to draw. I thought certain words—like "doodle"—blocked people from awareness of entering into a profound, intuitive process when they draw.

Connie said, "Why don't you call it *stream drawing*?" Her solution made perfect sense to me. It is the best way to describe what is really going on when we draw with ease and open flow, tapping into our stream of consciousness and creative source. I realized at that moment that I had found the perfect replacement for the d-word! Thank you, Connie and Polly!

Drawing is a fundamentally transformative personal process. We need to use good language to describe it, or we risk missing the gifts it can give us. Maybe it is time to take drawing more seriously, as an act of personal and meaningful empowerment and something integral to our souls as individuals and members of humanity.

Changing the Tide:
How to Cultivate a Relaxed Attitude About Drawing

Though I hope to inspire you to avoid less-than-ideal terms like the d-word, there *is* a special power in not taking every mark too seriously. A mark maker, in order to experience the gratification of making a drawing with real emotion in it, need not be too precious about it. But I believe we can have a dignified way to describe drawing and still maintain a carefree, loose, and easy attitude. We can still enjoy that sense of freedom while making marks. One of my greatest teachers, the late artist Fred Gregory, used to make that exact point with us in art school. Nothing was more serious than drawing; yet we couldn't take a finished drawing too seriously. He taught us to draw with vine charcoal and wipe the drawings away after we created them. Vine charcoal is light and easy to smudge off, so only the ghost of the drawing remained, a light impression of what had once been bold marks. We would then start the next drawing on top, wipe it away, and continue working on the same piece of newsprint. Fred also had us rub out our paintings, too, during life study, to make the point that *the process was more important than the product.*

I learned from him that I have to be ready and willing to know that the experience of mark making is more important than the final product. Being overly precious and delicate about it does the artist no service. And so, I must admit, I realize that using silly-sounding words like the d-word to describe that loose way of drawing may allow us to feel more loose and free than if we used some formal term. "Doodle" might better describe our sense of joy and release while drawing; the d-word may have an upside.

Hopefully the term "stream drawing" will signal to you to breathe and truly go with the flow when you draw on napkins or on paper or on walls. The bottom line is, if we're relaxed, we draw better. If we feel no pressure or threat of criticism, we flow right into creative bliss: the brain is not in survival mode. When we are not self-conscious or uptight, the brain can function at its best. During stream drawing, we can revel in the power of the brain to charge up, while slipping into that creative zone that is so rewarding (no matter what we call it).

Drawings, whether on margins of paper or on the ceiling of the Sistine Chapel, have an infinite transformative power in them. Something profound happens when the hand, heart, and mind work in harmony. In my mind, those moments are the most promising and potentially enlightening. The process we undertake in creating these drawings is valuable. It is time to stop belittling a profoundly powerful action we have (literally!) at our fingertips.

We can use drawing to get into that creative, empathic place by taking it seriously and not too seriously, all at once. The *process of discovery* held in drawing is powerful and delivers us to our own uniqueness. Our acts of drawing provide opportunities for us to make discoveries we may not have made otherwise.

So let's get playful and forget the criticism and labeling. Let's be open to free expression. Drawing is a lot like dancing. You don't have to be "good" at dancing—or drawing—to benefit from it. It makes you feel great. It helps you celebrate your life.

Drawing Has a Multitude of Purposes

While exploring this intuitive process, it is good to remember that there are many ways to draw and different reasons to use drawing as a skill and tool. Drawing has always been a part of our history as humans; it is part of how we understand ourselves. Humankind has always used drawing to tell stories and describe our perceptions of our reality, from the first cave paintings to illustrative journalism. Drawing captures the truth of our existence, conveys emotion, and transmits information. All forms of drawing and painting are extremely valuable because they can deepen our emotional awareness, often bringing life to a subject even better than a photograph can.

A lot of people avoid attempting to draw because they believe or were taught that drawings must "look realistic." These realistic drawings—known as renderings—are valued for their exact (or close to exact) depiction of a person, place, or thing. As an artist, studying and visually describing people with light, shadow, and texture is sacred to me; yet, while realistically executed drawings (still lifes and portraits) are wonderful to create and behold, they are not the only valuable way to draw.

It is easy to understand how we came to think that drawing is "good" only when it realistically depicts a scene, event, or person's likeness and that it is "bad" when it fails to achieve this. A drawing does not always have to be judged a success or failure based on whether it is a good rendering. There are different kinds of drawings and the process is what matters, as well. A rendering won't feel good unless the artist is completely in the flow while creating it. Stream drawing is a great way to feel the relaxation necessary to make any kind of drawing.

Even serious realists know that the quality of life will be absent if they do not first approach drawing in a *loose and easy manner*. This is true, no matter how masterfully the art was executed. Therefore, the stream drawing method is one that benefits everyone, from those with personalities least inclined to be artistic to the creators of the most exquisite art on earth.

A Note About Intuition and Instinct

My hope is that this book will guide you in reclaiming the intuition that you naturally possess. In my personal experience, intuition and instinct are very closely connected. Mothers will tell you that there is truth to the saying "women's intuition" or "maternal instinct"—and fathers feel it as well. Many parents react instinctively to their surroundings, picking up signals from the environment as to whether or not their baby is safe. Often, this sense is a compelling inner force that asserts itself within the parent's physical being. In other words, before thinking or processing feelings, a parent responds in an intuitive way, based on an instinctive impulse. Think of mother bears, who instinctively charge anything that comes between them and their cubs.

Instinct is connected with intuitive knowledge because we intuit using our physical attributes. We are in a human body. Our body is what we use to gather information, express ourselves, and make choices as we move through life. Intuition, much like pure physical instinct, often alerts us to information before we register it logically. If we suppress our instincts, we usually pay the price. For example, if you were near a fireplace where the crackling pile of logs was slipping out of the grate, your instincts would probably alert you to stay away from the fire. If you ignored your instincts, you would be irritated with yourself if a spark flew and singed your pants. Worse, you could get burned because you ignored your instincts—*you knew* the logs were slipping and sparking.

In the same way, our intuitive knowing speaks to us through our body, mind, senses, and spirit. For example, while I was waiting to close on a house, I went to look for a rental to use as a temporary living space. The rental was on an island, and the water was across the road. My husband and I love living by the sea, so this seemed like a great idea. There was a boat launch just a few steps away from the house. It would have been a great place to stay until we moved into our new house. But when I stepped inside, I did not get a good feeling. I felt slightly ill at ease with a sagging kind of nervousness. Since we had very little time to secure a place, I shrugged off my instincts and intuition, and paid more attention to the logical reasons for why the house would be fine for us to rent. I told the real estate agent that we'd rent it and said, "It's for barely a month, anyway." But before I could sign the lease, another couple snagged it. They would be long-term renters, so the owners gave the lease to them instead. I felt only mild annoyance at this news. I didn't like the beach house rental much, so I didn't feel we'd lost something good. I shrugged it off and hurried to find another place. A few miles from the coast, we found another place and signed a lease. I noticed that this other rental felt a little better. I didn't register any feelings of anxiety—just a smell of moth balls and too much porcelain and glass to make it comfy.

A few weeks after my family had settled in, a major hurricane roared up the East Coast. It demolished many coastal homes, including the one I almost rented. The storm was so severe that the road near the beach house rental was battered; the bridge leading to it was closed. The boats in the harbor were piled on top of each other. The beach house rental took on water and loads of sand. My unsettled vibe had served me well. I felt charmed, as though we had been guided to a safer place by a benevolent force, even though I had pushed aside my own intuition.

I had done nothing to draw in this benevolence. In that situation, I had the intuitive-instinctive impression *not* to rent that beach house, but I did not honor my feelings; I did the opposite and agreed to rent it. We were spared the misery of the hurricane, flooding, and evacuation; I was lucky that the universe provided us with a different way.

I find that tuning in and consciously registering my intuition is easier and better when I use stream drawing as part of the process. Had I told the realtor, "We want to rent this beach house, but I need a few hours to think about it," gone home, and done a stream drawing to connect to my intuitive impressions, I might have allowed myself time to acknowledge what I was feeling. Instead, I left it up to fate and ignored my own intuitive, indwelling message. It is common sense to take time to reflect and pay attention to your gut feelings and intuitive notions that come your way. Drawing is a process that enables us to truly slow down, listen inwardly, and honor the information that surfaces. Looking back, I wish I had kept my sketchbook in the car that day. I could have sat behind the wheel and closed my eyes, asking: "Do I really think this beach rental is the smartest way to go? Is it the best decision for all concerned?"

I bet that, with the first mark made, I'd have had to face the fact that I had a sinking feeling about that place.

How Synchronicity Plays into Your Intuitive Discoveries

Stream drawing and intuitive sensing gives us a certain mobility that we would not otherwise have. Being intuitive and trusting the process keeps us in a progressive, positive flow. We see how delightfully easy it is to go through the day—not everything needs a push or force. We do not have to "make things happen" or constantly struggle to assert our plans. Intuition gives us bread crumbs (in the form of synchronistic messages) along the way that clue us in. When we listen to these messages, we don't feel stuck or blocked. I find it is a more interesting way to move through the day. Freedom of movement in our lives is evident when we acknowledge synchronistic events. If we stay in touch with our intuitive knowing, what we experience resonates and registers for us in lighthearted ways (such as when you think of someone and they call you at that same moment) or in more profound ways (such as when you get a hunch to fly home early from a trip and arrive just in time to rush a family member to the hospital). If I remember my dreams, I notice what the subconscious offers me; if something in my waking hours matches a detail in my dream, I certainly notice that, too. (For example, I recently had a dream in which a person I have not seen or heard from in many months was talking to me about a sense of dread she felt. This woman called me the very next day and told me she was worried about her mother. Synchronicity!) The same thing happens when I create a stream drawing, or do an intuitive stream drawing reading for a client. For example, prior to a session, I may see a drum appear in the drawing, and then the client arrives for the session and says, "Oh, I just started taking drum lessons!" Synchronicity abounds when we open to our intuitive ability to gather, process, and find meaning in our experiences. It can make a drab day more fun and a fun day, ecstatic. We are enriched by the sense that everything and everyone is actually connected, if we only notice. This sense in turn helps us to feel whole and centered and part of our surroundings. This is what it means to have emotional abundance.

Drawing Conclusions

We have a great opportunity, through drawing, to connect our conscious mind with the unconscious and discover who we are and how we came to be who we are. Drawing is a natural way to understand ourselves more deeply. Through drawing, we can emote, create, respond, and perceive all at once, with awareness and compassion. Enjoying our perceptions and creative source, we experience a heightened sense of connectedness with our environment and with those around us as we relate to others, creating our lives anew moment by moment. Our innate ability to draw is something to celebrate and honor. It is a way of activating the total mind as it works in unity. We no longer shy away from mark making. Through drawing, we get a chance to see what no longer works for us; we can let go of ideas we no longer need as we gain new insights that better nurture us. Life is not a series of separate bits that we have to spend decades sorting through to make sense of, but rather, it is a wonderfully evolving kaleidoscope of thoughts and feelings, of actions and responses, fueled by creative will. The design of life is ever changing and magical. We see how we truly are a part of everything. Stream drawing lets us invite our intuitive knowing or inner voice to guide us. Following that pathway toward unconscious, empathic, and intuitive intelligence can make each day feel like a fresh beginning. Drawing to raise our creative consciousness helps us become aware of happy synchronicities and unexpected connections in our ordinary days. These signs and messages guide and enlighten us through serious and lighthearted moments alike.

Stream Drawing:
Getting into the Flow

Stream-of-consciousness drawing, or "stream drawing," expresses the unconscious onto paper, the way dreams bring up images and emotion for us on a mental screen. To get into this flow, we have to allow ourselves to relax into intuitive processing. How we *feel* when we let ourselves go into that zone—where we're making a mark that is one continuous line—is even more important than what arrives on the paper. Stream drawing lets the artist allow feelings and thoughts to open up while the relaxed hand is making marks. Letting go of the outcome and of our need to rationally comprehend input and what's happening is what being intuitive is about.

The marks we make in this relaxed, stream drawing state may feel delightful or may be surprising. During a stream drawing session, something quietly pleasant may surface or it may be something enormous. Shifting toward using the intuitive brain and allowing the logical brain to release control for a time allows us to solve problems and reach new insights through intuitive discovery. The intuitive mind and heart are given the breath of life. Even if nothing much happens—just a few moments of altered emotions or thoughts—that is worthwhile. We can't listen to our intuition if we have the same thoughts constantly hammering our minds.

While doing these stream drawings and developing my technique for intuitive stream drawing readings, my entire presence shifts. I shift from using mainly my rational and logical mind to being more conscious of intuitive messages and insights on a daily basis. Stream drawing allows me to transform my thoughts and emotions into ideas and new perceptions. I personally experience intuition as a blend of empathy (feeling for and sensing the worth of others, the idea we are all connected as humans), imagination (a sense of wonderment and curiosity that is exciting, gratifying, and powerful to explore), creativity (what we do to generate and produce expressions propelled by our emotions and imagination), and spirituality (a deep feeling of bliss that suggests to me that I am part of an unseen mystery more powerful than myself). Stream drawing brings it all together. As lines on paper take form, images emerge. I actively transform my mood, and my heart literally feels lighter. Often, new ideas come up. I am able to relax more and enjoy myself as I allow my intuition to sort out life, instead of trying to control or define my world with logic. Being intuitive in this way is a pathway to creative discovery!

Recently, I was contacted by Israeli psychiatrist Dr. Pinki Feinstein, who was researching this sensation of creative release that happens when people get into a stream-of-consciousness flow. We spoke about a painting program he developed called "Intuitive Painting." He noticed that using the logical mind without the intuitive mind (the left side of the brain is associated with rational and logical thought, while the right side of the brain is the intuitive, creative side) shuts down learning. Using the intuitive, creative side, as we do in drawing in a stream-of-consciousness state, is vital. He explained, "During these moments, the mind is getting free of pressure. The creative right brain is allowed to enter the scene and begins to connect the dots of all cognitive material that was perceived by the left, rational side of the brain. For maximal effect, swinging between the left and right sides of the brain as they work together is optimal."*

---

*Dr. Pinkie Feinstein (creator of Intuitive Painting), in emailed discussion with the author, 2013.

A Dual Purpose:
Stream Drawing and Intuitive Stream Drawing Readings

I see stream drawing as having two functions. The first is to learn how to draw in the flow, without blocking yourself. In this kind of drawing, you surrender mentally and emotionally to express yourself on paper using your body, hand, and pencil. This allows the rational and intuitive sides of the brain to open wide and work together, back and forth. The practice is gratifying and can be used as often as you like, on any given day, and as a lifelong practice. You can use it to enhance your sense of well-being and for centering and processing thought and feeling, personal unconscious memory and associations.

The second function is to use the method to do an intuitive stream drawing reading. In this use of stream drawing, you draw with a particular concern or question for yourself or on behalf of another person. Afterward, you can peer into the drawing in order to gain insight. Intuitive stream drawing reading takes the stream drawing practice to a deeper intuitive realm. There is a structure to intuitive stream drawing readings consisting of four stages that are easy and natural to follow. But first, you need to stretch and play while stream drawing, for sheer pleasure. Once you feel good about stream drawing and know how to use it to get into your creative, intuitive flow, we will begin practicing intuitive stream drawing readings.

Warm Up Before You Create a Stream Drawing

First, to feel loose and in the flow while drawing, experiment with noticing how it feels to draw simple lines across paper. This may seem like a restricting kind of thing, the opposite of getting into a flow—like wanting to dance freely but being asked to walk ten miles in a straight line—but it actually feels good to do. When you get started, notice how to use *pressure* to *express emotion*. You'll draw lines that are heavy (pushing down hard with your pencil) and light lines (using less pressure). After warming up this way, your stream drawing technique will feel even more amazing. You will feel the tension in your gestures and awaken to the subtle release you get from varying the pressure of making marks, pencil to paper. It is very sensual. You'll feel the contrast of being limited to drawing in a straight line versus drawing as randomly as possible.

You can use this form of expression and meditation as often as you like. You are about to open up to a new method of intuitive knowing and sensing. So this first step is fundamentally important for progressing and eventually conducting intuitive stream drawing readings. These are the necessary steps to take to get into your stream drawing flow:

- Getting paper and pencil ready
- Loosening up the body, arms, and hands
- Using your nondominant hand as well as your dominant one
- Drawing with complete ease and feeling good doing it
- Closing your eyes to get into a meditative state while stream drawing

Get your body ready: you don't want to be stiff or feel uncomfortable. Drawing appears to be something only the hand and fingers are engaged in, but actually we use the entire body, arms and shoulders, back and neck. So take a deep breath and stand up. Do some large, circular motions with your arms to get them really limber and ready to go. Stretch your neck gently and swivel your hips. You should feel anything *but* uptight. Generally, I find that I'm holding tension in my body and don't even realize it. Some stretches help me notice ways in which I may be stiff or inflexible.

Have your blank piece of paper ready (eight-by-ten inches or larger, please) on a steady surface. Grab a pencil or charcoal and sit comfortably. Take your pencil in your nondominant hand. Breathe in a few times, slowly and deeply. Rotate your wrists in little circles, keeping a loose, light grip on the pencil. And you're ready!

Try It! Experiment with Line Gradation

As I described, you'll experiment with drawing lines as a way to sensitize yourself to what it really feels like to move a pencil across paper, *influencing your lines with emotion as you draw them*. You'll use pressure and speed while making these lines.

Using your dominant hand for this first exercise (and keeping your eyes open for now), hold the pencil point at one end of the paper. Draw a single line straight across the paper. It doesn't matter whether it's actually straight or not; chances are, it will not be a perfectly straight line. The point is not to make perfectly straight lines but rather to create many lines to get into the feel of drawing marks. This will condition your muscles. Your shoulders, arm, and hand muscles are required to work in concert for you to draw loosely.

Make up to five lines, one after another. Watch as each one goes across the page, from left to right. Notice if you're relaxed or uptight; breathing or holding your breath. Be aware of how you feel and try to be as comfortable as possible while drawing.

After making these first five straight lines across the paper (don't worry if they're not totally straight!), draw your next line (with closed eyes) by *pressing down hard* and then *gradually lifting and softening* so that your one continuous line is dark and then light (see Figure 2). Change from bearing down to drawing lightly, with much less pressure. Do several lines, one beneath the other, using a varying amount of pressure in each line. Observe the variations between dense and dark line pressure to light-as-air line pressure. Notice how you feel while creating these lines. Does it feel good to draw pressing down hard or better when you use a lighter hand? Does it feel good transitioning from pressing hard with your pencil to using less pressure? Or does it feel better using less pressure at first as you draw the line, then switching to using more pressure?

It is important to notice how you *feel* while creating lines with gradation because drawing is all about getting a feel for the marks you are making and noticing what feels inwardly good to draw. We know when it feels good to sing high or sing low, so think of drawing as similar to that—you are singing with your pencil as it streams across the page. The line begins to take on a type of personality. It may convey a message. The line is dark (like singing a low note). Then it is lighter (like singing a high note), and before you know it, you have something more than just a basic straight line. A sort of language is conveyed by the line as it emerges from the gesture of your hand. And closing your eyes helps you feel it.

Figure 2.
Line gradation experiment.

Next, using your dominant hand, draw with line gradation but also go *slow or fast* (alternate keeping your eyes closed and open). You may bear down hard while starting a line, going slowly to feel the pressure last. Or you may begin with a line so light, it is barely a whisper on the page; this line may be drawn faster. Experiment with line gradation and speed, making a few more lines. (You may turn the sheet over or get another one, if you like).

Now that you're aware of the physical, seductive sensation of making marks, it's time to stream draw with total abandon!

Try It! Frozen Pond Exercise

The frozen pond drawing is a way to get into that blissful flow you deserve to feel. Get a piece of blank paper and take your pencil in hand. Try drawing using line gradation and varying speeds while imagining you are skating across a frozen pond. The blank paper is a wonderful, pristine pond; your hand and your pencil are the skater. Take a deep breath and feel as comfortable as you can. Breathe in and out, loosening your shoulders, arm, and wrist as you work with a loose and easy feeling.

Using the hand you normally use to write or draw, close your eyes as you draw all over the frozen pond (blank paper). Use one continuous line that meanders and slides all about the space. You may feel yourself doing figure eights or satisfying loops and turns; your line may zigzag or turn sharply. Or both! You may draw fast or slow, press hard or let up on the pressure. Continue this one lovely line as it creates shapes all over the page, envisioning yourself as the skater on ice. See Figure 3 for an example.

Create as many of these frozen pond drawings as you like. (I recommend doing dozens!) Draw one continuous line that does whatever you'd like it to—or whatever it seems to want to do! Draw across and around blank pieces of paper. Use both sides of the paper, and get the most out of each piece for this warm-up exercise. As you draw with varying line gradation and varying speeds, notice how you feel. What does your arm or hand feel? What do you feel inside, emotionally, while skating around on the ice? Do you feel more relaxed than you did prior to drawing? Do you feel any other notable sensations?

Figure 3.
Frozen pond drawing exercise.

Try It! Use Your Opposite Hand

Now, with your eyes closed, try both of the above exercises—the line gradation and frozen pond—with your less dominant hand, the one you do not normally use while writing or drawing. You may discover you feel more out of control while using the opposite hand to draw, or you might feel more free and uninhibited, or a combination of both! Most of the drawing you will do in this book will involve using your less dominant hand, partly because it is easier to be loose and emotive with the hand that has less physical control. Since this book is about using drawing to access personal unconscious memory and intuitive sensing, using the opposite hand is optimal.

Drawing Conclusions

In this chapter, you've embarked on your stream drawing adventure, creating stream drawings that will ultimately prepare you for creating intuitive stream drawing readings. You have created straight lines to acquaint yourself with the subtle changes in pressure when applying pencil to paper. You've warmed up and loosened up, allowing your logical mind to relax and your intuitive, creative mind to express. You've experimented more with line gradation (tension and variation of pencil contact with the paper) and noticed how you felt while drawing as well as conveying feeling and thoughts as they streamed through you, expressing them onto paper.

You've begun a process of communicating through drawing, welcoming the unconscious to flow into awareness. And you've given both your dominant and nondominate hand a chance to get into the flow, allowing the rational and intuitive aspects of mind to cocreate. You've skated over a frozen pond, creating all kinds of marks with one continuous line. The next step is to have some fun *looking* at lines and shapes to see what messages they give us or what feelings they convey. This will help you develop a visual-intuitive way of seeing and sensing. It will better prepare you for intuitive stream drawing readings, drawing to capture emotions, and gaining deeper empathy and intuitive insights.

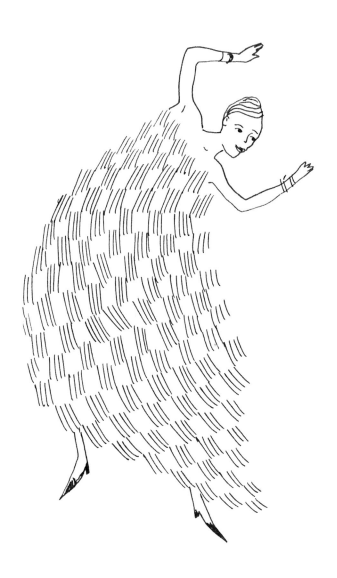

3

Playing with Your Perception of Line

In this chapter, you'll explore the ways in which mark making is natural to humans, but also how it is natural for humans to respond to marks once they're made. We have an innate urge to make our marks, and we also have a brilliant capacity for making sense of marks made, by perceiving and forming ideas about them. We have experiences, we make marks in response to them, and then we decide what the marks mean. Being intuitive allows us to do more than just rationally identify drawn marks: "This one is straight; that one is curly." We can emotionally respond to them: "This one is making me feel cautious; that one is making me feel excited."

Finding meaning and expression in drawn lines and shapes is an artistic and intuitive process that will help you develop a visual-intuitive language that is your very own. This is a building process that is natural but not always cultivated. In our day-to-day lives, we are prepared to give facts and logical answers more than we are asked or expected to provide our own take on things. We are good at offering generalizations that describe our collective, universal meanings, but not as often given the opportunity to zero in on our personal, unconscious meanings. This exercise is a chance to reflect on what things mean to you personally, expanding your process of discovery. In other words, each time you see a line (curvy, straight, looping, zigzag—any kind of line), you'll be recognizing it as a form of visual expression and communication. You'll register what a line and its visual expression or character conveys or suggests to you personally. An example of my own is that I was looking at a line recently and noted that it was shaped like a swooping arch that dipped down low and curved, with a loop in it. I said to myself, "That line has such a swooping curve and a big egg-shaped loop in it." I was already beginning to register an emotional response to the drawing. Then I said to myself, "And it makes me feel seasick! It reminds me of the time I was on a rollercoaster and regretted it because I didn't enjoy it at all. I felt out of control." Describing a line by what it feels like and what it reminded me of helps me open my intuitive sensibility. It helps me see how the line talks to me personally. The main emotion I had when viewing this particular line was that of feeling unnecessarily out of control. I reflected a little more and realized that I had learned to accept that there are certain things others may enjoy that I do not; seeing this line and intuiting its meaning helped me revisit a particular concept I had discovered based on an experience from my past.

Developing a perceptual, emotional response to drawing is a way to set about creating your very own visual-intuitive language. The visual part of your language perceives a line and the form it takes. The next time you see a familiar swooping line, you'll remember that you have seen this shape before. Then you can immediately recognize what it means to you. The intuitive part senses the meaning the line has to offer you according to your own life experiences, thoughts, feelings, and associations. You'll build your "vocabulary," making new meanings each time you look at that line or one that is similar to it. Because line-work is so varied, you will never reach a moment when you have gathered all there is to know or feel.

By practicing this method of perceiving lines and shapes as they interact, you will gradually develop intuitive seeing as a second nature. But to get there, you must go through the process and make seeing this way a practice. Then you will slowly build a visual-perceptual language that holds within it an awareness of your responses, personal meanings, and intuitive knowing. The following examples of lines and shapes will help you create that language through experience. If you listen inwardly with each visual presentation of line and form in this exercise, you will deepen your empathic sensing; this will serve you while you're learning to do intuitive stream drawing readings. This is about seeing differently—with a visual perception that is intuitive in nature. Cultivating this visual skill will support you in living an intuitive life. Developing this visual language is a playful, enjoyable process of discovery, because *art is subjective and relative* to each of us. Art and a visual comprehension of line, shape, texture, color, and form provides for you a window to your soul. Let yourself journey to the place within you where so much can be discovered.

A New Vision: "Gaze" and "Trust Your Words"

Now that we've experimented with the basics of stream drawing, we can begin to use this carefree drawing technique in a new and purposeful way: intuitive stream drawing readings. Before we do that, though, we'll take steps toward seeing and understanding, two methods I call "Gaze" and "Trust Your Words."

⤳▷ Gaze

When we look at an object, the impulse is to immediately label it. Gazing is different, in that there is no expectation. A label isn't necessarily the outcome; labeling is not as important as considering the object with a completely open mind. Gazing means looking in a relaxed and "off-task" way—seeing the image without having to define it correctly or rationally. It allows you to suspend judgment and to accept whatever arises in your conscious mind. Gazing is a way to visually encounter a person, place, or thing while your own truths gradually surface. Feelings and associations may drift in and out while gazing, as well as totally new ideas about the subject you are perceiving.

This is how gazing works: Open your eyes once you've stopped drawing. Take a deep breath and gaze at your drawing. Gazing in this context implies looking intently, but with an open mind and heart. Once you become relaxed while gazing and develop a quiet sense of presence, you will open to your empathic, intuitive knowing. While absorbing the image you have made with a sense of gratitude and ease, you will begin to discover a feeling of enchantment so pleasant that you may feel yourself light up from head to toe. Feeling this wonderment is the sign that you are activating your "higher self," your spirit within. This aspect of self is your total sense of well-being that is *a state of being* which resides in you *perpetually*, even if you block or do not recognize it. This aspect of you is already complete, enriched, and open to heartfelt information. Stream drawing and gazing allow you to unblock and feel the deep beauty that is the natural state at the core of your being.

As you practice gazing, take all of the visual imagery you created *inward* without focusing on anything in particular at first—gazing is about seeing with an expectant openness. Try to be just as aware of what you see in your *peripheral* vision as what you see at your focal point. Gazing allows for appreciation and an empathic but detached observance. When you gaze, behold the image with an open heart. You may have feelings that are similar to those you felt while creating the stream drawing. Just appreciate the marks you made, allowing thoughts to stream in and back out. As you gaze, notice if you reflexively criticize or label your drawing; let those thoughts flutter away from you like butterflies. Breathe. Do not criticize yourself or listen to your inner chatter at all. Quiet your mind without judging your drawing; instead, gaze at it with real gratitude. These are the marks you made. They are evidence of your free will on planet Earth, evidence of your power to create change on a subtle level.

Trust Your Words

Trust whatever comes into consciousness while gazing, knowing there is no right or wrong. Allow feelings and meanings to arrive and accept them.

This is how it works: practice trusting what streams in from your unconscious to your conscious mind. This is exciting because you can feel surprised and delighted by what arrives. Ideas seem to stream in from nowhere! Trusting your impressions encourages your mind toward creative possibilities and gives you the opportunity to entertain different perspectives. Free association of thought and feeling is a wild ride, since you do not know where your thoughts will take you.

It is necessary to practice this because we have a tendency to mistrust ourselves. We block or resist our instincts, and judge or examine thoughts before we commit to them with spoken words. We analyze before allowing our intuitive thoughts into an internal belief system. We reflexively label the things we look at (that's a tree, that's a shoe, that's a tiger, etc.), so we are rarely in an intuitive flow while looking at people, places, or things. We are often locked in a logical, rational mind-set. In this intuitive exercise we are going to decide that whatever surfaces in our minds while gazing can be a guide—an intuitive guide, and it does not have to be logical.

You do not have to do away with logic. In fact, you will use some logic while gazing. Naturally, your mind will try to find what is recognizable. You don't have to fight it; this is part of this process. You may see a line or loop that reminds you of something your mind understands easily, such as a line that looks like a stick or a square shape that reminds you of a table. The point is not to block your rational thoughts or your intuitive ones. Practice not blocking anything that comes to mind. You may look at a line that reminded you of a stick and end up having words surface into your conscious mind that do not seem logically related. It might suddenly remind you of a person you used to know named LeRoy. Why? That's the fun part. You will use your visual-intuitive language and answers will come via intuitive sensing, just as they often arrive in a logical context.

Trusting your words is easy. You just have to open up to your intuitive intelligence and your emotional, empathic awareness, which is part of your intuitive knowing. It is not only fun, but also a fascinating experience. This method of self-discovery works when you use visual marks to create intuitive, unconscious associations. We each have a history that is unique. We carry within us the information we got from all these life experiences, and we can tap into that information when we respond to images. This inner core is where your intuitive intelligence resides. And the best way to tap into this amazing source and essence of knowledge is to get playful, like a child. Having a playful attitude and disposition is what makes self-discovery so much fun. As a result, your imaginative, creative expressiveness blossoms, heightening your sensitivity.

Lines Are People, Too!

The "personality" of a line can be seen and felt by the viewer. A line has character in its quality, determined by its attributes, such as its shape, density, length, and angle.

The most simple line—for example, a check mark on a grocery list—has an entire universe of personality in it, giving us clues about the mark's temperament. As we observe a line's personality, we determine and ascribe meaning to it. Each of us, individually, assigns our own meaning. For example, I may look at a check mark and see a very rigid and energetic shape. It is exacting and positive. It gives me the feeling of "I mean business"—like a person that wastes no time. Someone else may see and feel completely different things when looking at the same mark. It might remind them of a line graph showing how well the stock market is doing (it starts at a low height, plummets down, then quickly rises up very high). We each have our own perceptions, and lines will teach us what they are and what they mean to us personally if we pay attention.

The lines we draw speak to us! In this section, we are going to play, using simple drawings to discover the essence of each line. You will have a chance to frolic with your responses in a lighthearted way, letting your imagination sail. This will help you understand feelings that arise when you stream draw and will be greatly helpful while conducting intuitive stream drawing readings.

Truly, even in a very simple mark, a world of information can be discovered. Just as a single note of music can fill us with emotion or a single scent can immediately elicit a strong memory, lines and marks stimulate our feelings. It is important for us to understand our responses to images, because once we are attuned to our own associations, we respond intuitively, with conscious awareness. Intuitive stream drawing work or other kinds of psychic reading is possible as we build our awareness and an inner structure of *consciousness stemming from our own meanings* (our own associations and personal unconscious memory based on our unique history), but we have to become sensitive in order to truly value all the information we carry inside us. These exercises were created to help you see how meanings arise from visual clues. Your experience will inform and guide you. Remember, it is not a formula, but a process.

Drawing the Line: Content and Context—How Lines Talk to Us

Drawn lines and marks carry a body of content that we each understand in our own way, depending on our perception. We use our five senses to give context, or meaning, to everything we encounter. Art forms such as lines and shapes represent elements from our experiences in the world, either symbolically or literally. It is up to us to understand and comprehend the personal meanings in art forms. To develop a visual-intuitive language, we embark on a journey to discover and know *what our own meanings are* and how to use them to have a better life.

Projection and the Role It Plays in Our Perceptions

As we begin our next visual-intuitive adventure, I want to introduce projection, which plays a big part in the process of stream drawing. Projection is a response we send outward to all things in our environment. As we perceive, we project our own ideas about a subject directly onto it. In other words, I project my own experiences on what I perceive around me. I may project outwardly that something is "good" or "bad," but that doesn't make it necessarily true—yet it may be true to me. An example of this is that I got a very short haircut and loved it. I was so excited and felt so free. I encountered someone later that day who saw my haircut and instantly assumed my short hair meant that I was unhappy. *She projected onto me what it would feel like to her if she resorted to a short haircut.* To her it was a sign of depression or of troubling times; possibly she only cut her hair when she felt upset. But for me, it symbolized freedom and artistic expression that took me years to be gutsy enough to demonstrate!

Projection is part of perception for each of us, and being aware of it will help us to look beyond what we currently perceive. While we accept our own truths as they arrive, we also keep an open heart and mind so that we can gain new insights. Reflecting while gazing and trusting the words as they come (meanings we assign to visual stimuli) involves projection. We see images and project our own meaning onto them; it's a natural reaction and relationship between vision and mental processing. Our memories influence us enormously and quickly offer us input as we form our perceptions of what we see, sending those perceptions outward as projections. At all times we have the conscious, preconscious, and unconscious (or subconscious) working with us, helping us determine what things mean to us. Memories are available for retrieval through the stream of consciousness.

In my first book on intuition, a working journal using forty large image cards, I made the point that imagery can powerfully seize memories from the unconscious mind and project them at faster-than-light speed into our awareness. A single image can suddenly cause us to feel and remember something we forgot we knew. Other sensory exposure besides sight can do this, too, such as music or smelling the scent of something from childhood, like your grandmother's perfume. Encountering the same scent can take you back decades as it delivers a memory you didn't realize you had, yet it was there all the time! Experiences bring it all back into conscious recognition.

Beneath the Conscious Mind

We know what is on the open sea of the conscious mind, but there is much more under the surface. Interpretations and perceptions stored within the unconscious mind appear in conscious awareness when something triggers a memory. Those memories can be pleasant or unpleasant. But even if an experience is long forgotten, it can be brought back into the arena of the conscious mind, depending on the nature of the experience.

When experiences are unpleasant, we may not remember them for a number of reasons. The preconscious plays the role of the built-in protector, kind of like a mediator between the conscious and unconscious. Certain traumatic experiences sink below our level of consciousness because remembering them would mean experiencing the trauma all over again. Those forgotten memories are still there, streaming deeply through the mental-emotional layer under the threshold of our awareness. The preconscious mind sifts through what we can handle at any given time, and so certain memories may remain submerged in the subconscious while others enter fully into the mind. If repressed memories are too difficult for the ego (our persona, our sense and idea of self that we create in order to survive), then that stream of information will remain in the preconscious mind. We may not have developed the strength to incorporate, process, and cope with the information it holds, especially in the case of trauma or injury.

Psychic acceptance of this material (held back from the ego) is known as ego syntonic condition. Reflection and contemplation, prayer and meditation are a few ways in which the memory content can be brought out. Dreams and activities like expressive mark making and stream drawing are practices that can allow us to bring forward information from our subconscious mind. We need only to open ourselves to the stream of inner-knowing residing within. Through our empathic surrender, hidden and forgotten knowledge may flow, offering information that has the potential to be life-changing.

Activating this enormous stream of memory can feel very good, even when the memories are difficult for us, because our preconscious mind is there, protecting us. When we are ready to accept certain memories, it can be like an epiphany; we realize what caused us to be oriented in a certain way, or what motivated us in certain situations. Sometimes we break through barriers that have held us back in life.

While we stream draw and gaze, trusting our words (as memories and associations we hold), we *project* those impressions forward. Mark making is an act of will and intent—evidence of our presence and an expression of our gestures. We project further by creating lines and shapes on a previously blank page. Then, we read our own understandings of our drawings, intuiting meaning from the way lines and shapes interact and appear on the paper. As each of us is unique, we will have our own perceptions in addition to agreeing on universal or collective perceptions. For example, we may all agree that the glowing sphere in the night sky is the moon; we all see the moon in the sky. Yet, according to my personal experience, my definition of the moon may include my memory of reading folktales, fairy tales, or myths. So when I see the moon, my personal impressions are at play, whether I'm conscious of them or not. To another person, the moon may suggest space exploration or memories of wanting to be an astronaut. So, even though we collectively agree and recognize the moon, we will each have a unique experience when we look up at the moon. When we honor that stream of consciousness that delivers us these meanings—a source of compassion, information, and intuitive sensing—we connect with others in a more meaningful way as well.

Rainbow of Intuition: Synthesis of Perceptions

Our senses work together to give us a full range of information about the world around us. To explore that, we'll practice synthesis of the senses. We can claim our unique perceptions of how drawn lines make us think or feel. Not only will we look at lines, but we'll see how our unconscious memories and personal library of associations arise when we gaze.

For example, a single arcing line may remind you of a rainbow (the *context* being that a prism in the sky has this shape). Then your mind may immediately jump to the various *content* the image of an arc or rainbow has, such as memories of seeing a rainbow with family or friends. Immediate associations loaded with sensory input may add volume to the content as your awareness increases and builds on the original impression. First, you see an arc; then, you imagine a rainbow; then, you taste rainbow sherbet. A simple line shaped like an arc stimulated associations with the sense of sight and taste (*seeing* the rainbow and then thinking of the *flavor* of ice cream).

However, a line in the shape of an arc might hold completely different context and content for someone else. Perhaps she sees the arc as a bridge, which might take her back to memories of a bridge she used to cross frequently; she may remember the *scent* of mossy brook water. To another person, that same arcing line might remind him of a frown painted on a clown in a circus he once saw, bringing up the *sounds* of circus music and the ringmaster's voice. And in another person's mind, the line might produce a thought or feeling that *has no rational explanation*, where the context is not obviously connected and the content seems illogical.

We may not always be able to explain why images give us certain feelings or why intuitive sensing clues us into things (as in precognition), but we do know it happens. Art often elicits what we can't explain verbally, and intuitive knowing arrives similarly—seemingly out of nowhere. The important thing is to accept whatever surfaces, whether it is rational or not.

Try It! Get a Sense

Look at each drawing in Figure 4 and answer the sensory questions.

What would I smell like?

What would I sound like?

What would I feel like?

What would I taste like?

Figure 4.
Sensory Lines.

Perceiving the Message: Context and Content

For this exercise, we will practice being open to context and content. We'll let imagery awaken our five senses and put a human touch on each line we see. Imagine the lines you see as people, full of personality in their gestures.

While looking at the lines, write down what each type of line makes you feel or think. Do not hesitate or second-guess your associations. Write down whatever comes to you when you see and perceive these lines.

Become aware of your breathing. As you breathe slowly and deeply, gazing, relax into the image before you. Use the *gaze* technique (your intuitive seeing skill) as you consider the lines and questions in Figure 5. Enjoy the lines for what they are.

Comparing each line, think of their individual characteristics and get into a dialogue with yourself. "One line is like steps, the other is like a slide," you may say to yourself. Their attributes lead us to further descriptions as we gaze at them. The first question prompts: "Which one is going up?" I may respond without hesitation that the line that resembles a staircase feels as though I am going "up." The angle of the line beside it, higher on the left and lower on the right end, suggests "down" to me. Those single drawn lines speak volumes. Continue to gaze at the lines and absorb the feelings each one gives you, using your sense of logic to help you connect with them. No answer you give is wrong.

As you gaze at the other line exercises, ask yourself why you have arrived at your answers. Within them is information about how you perceive; your response, whether logical or more intuitive, is the key. The question "Which one is water?" compares a wavy line to a choppy one, shapes jutting up and back down. Logically, we might decide that the wavy line suggests ocean waves or ripples we have seen on the surface of water. Yet the other image could be frozen water, with rigid ice formations. Looking again, we might say that the wavy lines make us feel a particular rhythm and flow that we connect with swimming in the sea. Embrace whatever impressions arise when you gaze at the lines. Remember to play. Imagine these lines as people; build on this by having an inner dialogue about it. Also, remember to ask yourself questions about the lines and what they may mean. Be flexible. Playful

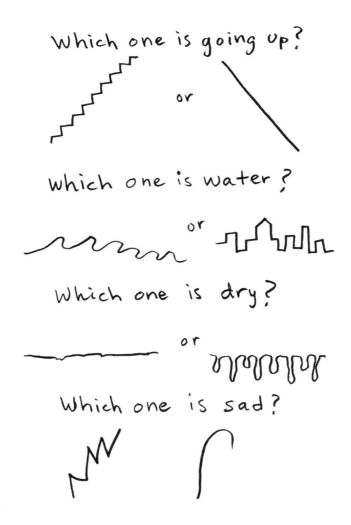

Figure 5.
Line drawing comparison, part one.

questions may help you relate to the lines as people. Think of roles people play in life and apply them to the lines you see. For example, given its visual characteristics, which line seems to project sadness? If so, why? Ask someone else what they see in these lines and have a fun discussion. Comparing and contrasting your impressions and projections can be exciting.

Now take some time to gaze at the lines in Figure 6 and allow your logic to help you as you accept your response. Then go deeper by asking yourself why and how you arrived at your answers.

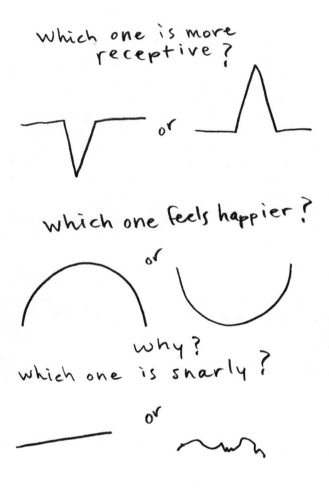

Figure 6.
Line drawing comparison, part two.

Your thinking may go like mine. For example, the question "Which one is more receptive?" is interesting for me because I perceive the first line on the left as jutting into the ground. To me, it looks like a deep cut into a surface. I could pour something into it if I wanted to. The line makes me feel a kind of receptivity, although it is a non-emotional line for me; I imagine its metallic precision, so I do not feel relaxed gazing at it. I feel a rigidity that I do not associate with the word "receptive." These lines, if human-like, would be more like robots than actual people, if you ask me. They might be beaky, hard-nosed personalities.

Looking again at the line on the left, I see it is concave (valley) and conveys spacial receptivity; therefore, it is receptive. I can drop or pour something in there. In contrast, the same line inverted the opposite way (on the right) makes me feel like I just encountered a steep hill. I do not perceive this line to be receptive at all. For me, it has a convex (peak), unyielding, industrial feeling. Breathing slowly to really take in this line, I think, maybe it *is* receptive, but in a way I didn't realize at first. Gazing for depth of meaning, I find that this convex line may be receptive in its own way. Perhaps it is a radio tower or satellite receiver of some kind, receiving unseen signals. I realize that if I go under it, I could fill that space, too—it looks hollow. Maybe it has a military purpose and is bombproof.

Try It! Gaze for Yourself

Gaze at the lines in Figure 7 and have fun with them. Read each question and allow your answers to surface. Then, gaze at each line separately to see how you feel. Think about them in terms of their characteristics: as masculine versus feminine, soft or hard, sharp or smooth. Does a line give you a feeling of calm or nervousness? Does one line seem angry? Take your time while you gaze. A line may suggest happiness or sadness, threat or safety, clarity or confusion. It depends how you relate to their expression. Breathe in and register why you have certain perceptions, and connect with your feelings.

As I gaze, my feelings begin to activate. Once I allow myself to go beyond my first responses, my imagination helps me discover my personal viewpoints, logical or not. There are many ways to perceive the lines, so enjoy gazing and contemplating them, discovering your own personal reactions and responses.

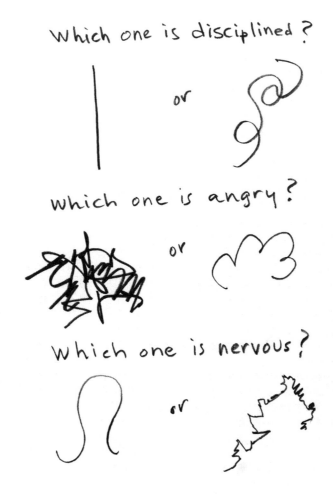

Figure 7.
Line drawing comparison, part three.

Try It! Drops in the Ocean: Multiple Lines Creating One Whole Form

As we discussed at the beginning of this section, lines and all other forms have a context and carry with them a body of content that we understand each in our own way
(depending on our perception). In this next image of several lines together (Figure 8),

you may find that your response to it is immediate. You may see something whole. It is made of many separate parts, all working together. These simple lines together take on a significant form. The content of the image allows you to describe it as a whole; the context allows you to arrive at the meaning you give it. While these meanings are subjective and personal, they can also be universal. The mind and heart seek and identify their meanings. Notice the image as a whole, then pay attention to each line and notice what they tell you.

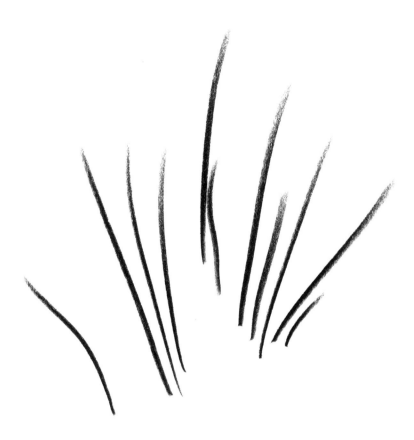

Figure 8.
Line drawing comparison of many lines together.

Gaze at this group of lines. You have already compared and contrasted sets of two lines—now try this one! This multi-line image offers another way to perceive the personality of a line. When more lines are seen together, arranged as a group, some different kinds of associations may come into play. What do they make as a whole? Are they all alike, or do they vary in expression? Several lines fanned out slightly might remind you of something in particular. Gazing at each line may offer you more insight into the personality of each one. The space between lines, called the negative space, may also hold information. Is one line far apart from another? Does that imply emotional distance? Is another line extremely close? Does that imply physical or emotional attachment of some kind?

Trust your words as you honor any and all associations you have while looking at the image. For example, I see grass blades, but I am also reminded of a lion's mane. The lines make gestures that remind me of calligraphy, and even sports team logos. I see a *y* and a *v*. The two lines in the center seem to me to be like parent and child—they are closer together than the other lines, which sway away from the center.

Try It! See the Personality of Shapes

Shapes evoke emotion and trigger associations out of the unconscious and into our decision making process, the same way lines can. Using the same playful openness you used while gazing at lines, try shapes and lines together. See what arises into your awareness.

Gaze at the shape with a line attached to it in Figure 9 and consider its form. Is it a person at all for you, or something else? Could it be a part of an actual person (such as the head)? What thoughts arise in you when you look at this line? What kind of object does it remind you of?

Trust your words as you gather all of the thoughts and impressions that come to mind while gazing at this. One may seem more prominent than another.

At first I think of a deflating balloon on a string. It gives me a depressed feeling, like a big letdown. Then the next line has the same basic idea, but with a different visual result. Now the line goes up softly to a floating bubble shape. For me, it looks

Does this remind you of anything?

Look at the same basic idea arranged differently.

Which one feels more hopeful?

Figure 9.
A line and shape together.

like a balloon that is filled with helium. All is not lost: the party is not over! The impression I get feels much better, a feeling of positivity coming over me.

Gazing longer at this line and shape combination makes me want a piece of bubble gum for some reason: my sense of taste was activated when I looked at this, probably by the round shape of the drawing. Blowing pink bubbles reminds me of childhood days and gives me an easygoing feeling. Yet it also awakens this memory: someone had gum but not enough to go around. They wrapped a rock in a gum wrapper, so that when my sister opened it, she had a full-out tantrum. I remember feeling so sorry that my sister got tricked. I wanted her to be treated better but felt helpless, and just stood there chewing my own piece of bubble gum. With this simple shape, I can check in with my unique feelings and memories. They conjure up a lot for me internally.

Gaze at the two shapes in Figure 10 and see if you feel something different from the last exercise. How do you react while gazing at the oval shape, compared with the rectangular one above it? What sensations and emotions come to you? Do you feel secure when you confront this shape combination, or wary? What is the dynamic between the two shapes? Do their size differences have a connotation for you? Does bigger mean more powerful? Does smaller mean vulnerable? Gaze at the first combination for a while and see what memories or associations surface for you, then go to the next. Do different feelings arise?

Trust your words as they arrive from within and don't worry about whether they seems logical or rational. Often the feelings and memories that arise from seeing shapes, lines, color, and texture are connected to certain life experiences that seem unrelated to the shapes themselves. For example, I immediately noticed I was struggling to breathe when I saw the first image of the rectangle on top of the little oval. The weight of it really got me, but if I had not paid attention, I might have not noticed this. *Gazing*, breathing, and allowing myself to go beyond rational thinking helped me recognize an inner response I had.

The question asks, "Do you think the oval is oppressed?" This is a leading question, one that prompts the response "Yes, the little oval is being overtaken by this enormous rectangle. Help!" Looking again, I feel new fondness for the image. That little oval reminds me of a pure and perfect white stone I found on a beach in Cape Cod. It was smooth and looked like alabaster. Nothing could crush it. I think this little oval is carrying the rectangle, perhaps because the rectangle can't roll around like the oval can. Or the oval has a job lifting empty cardboard boxes. With this new

Figure 10.
Rectangle and oval comparison.

impression, I feel better and can breathe more easily. Looking at the image below, where the rectangle is beneath the oval, I get all new feelings and ideas. Do you? And the next image of two ovals together, does this image convey an entirely different relationship? Is there a sense of companionship and trust or interdependence and affection? Or something else?

Gaze now at this triangle shape (Figure 11). The center traingle has a very different expression from the one above it. What is the quality of the line in comparison to the shape above? Imagine this shape in an argument with the shape above it. Who would win and why? Does this triangle remind you of anything? Anyone?

Trust your words as you gaze at this shape. What words can you come up with to describe this triangle?

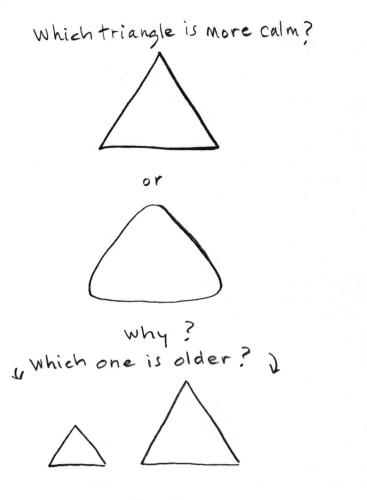

Figure 11.
Triangle comparison.

Gaze at the next triangles. These shapes have a few subtle differences. Concentrate on the small triangle. What happens when you gaze at this one in relation to the larger one? Is there a parental feel to these two triangles due to size differences? Or does it convey something else for you?

Remember the importance of being aware of the content and context. Take the time to notice how small variations communicate meaning to you; this is what helps you develop your visual-intuitive language. The soft-edged triangle may feel very different than the pointed one. When you finish gazing at the first two triangles, look at the two on the bottom. You might respond very quickly to the question asked about those two triangles. Ask yourself why you have the answer you have, and then play with options that might be possible as alternative ways to perceive the two together.

Trust your words as you write down whatever comes, without blocking or censoring yourself.

Let's put another line and shape together (Figure 12; see page 44). What kind of relationship do they have? Would they get along like the same things, or have different tastes altogether? What are their similarities and differences? Imagine that they are people. Do you have a pleasing feeling when you see them together, or something else? What do you make of the negative space, or the space between them? What does it convey, if anything? Does the negative space indicate intimacy or alienation? And what kind? Why or why not?

Trust your words as you consider the dynamic between these two shapes, and be playful!

Try It! Perceiving Lines and Shapes as Universal Messengers

There are some common, universally familiar configurations—often very simple ones—that we recognize immediately. We agree upon the meaning conveyed by the visual suggestion. Without even having time to consciously gaze at the image in Figure 13 (a single shape, a single line, and two short marks) we can see: this is a smiley face!

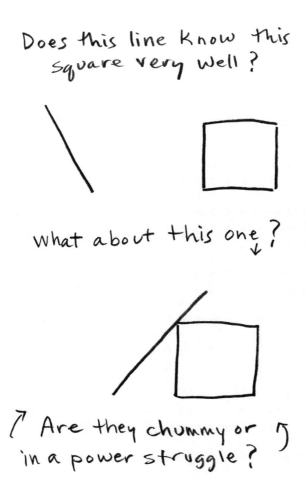

Figure 12.
Line and square shape together.

Gaze at the image at the top of the page in Figure 13. You may have discovered you did not even have to gaze—you immediately saw the circle, line, and marks and knew they were a face, mouth, and eyes. These simple marks most likely instantly registered meaning for you. And all we've done is play with a simple circle shape, a simple arc of a line, and two small marks.

Figure 13.
Smiley face, frowny face.

The same combination, with only one little change (inverting the arc) really alters the emotional response for me. Now I see a sad face instead of a smiley face.

Next, let's take the same shape, change the line from an arc to a straight line, and place it in a less logical position, atop the two small marks (see Figure 14), which I've moved a little closer to the line. What happens? It may no longer seem like a face, but can you intuit an emotion?

Figure 14.
Smiley brow.

Trust your words, any words that come to mind. Perhaps questions arise. Why do we even accept this as a human face? Nobody actually looks like this! If the marks for eyes were bigger, would you feel different about this face? (You can try this in your sketchbook or on a blank piece of paper.) Does this still look like a smiley face? Does it still have human characteristics? What emotions would this person be having? What happens when the line is moved to the center? Does the line speak to you in a completely different way now?

Gaze at variations of the same or similar lines, marks, and shapes. When we alter the arc line it can also change our conclusions about meaning and emotional content. Look at the personality change! Do you still see a face, no matter the arrangement? Do some combinations evoke radically disparate reactions from you? Does seeing a smile change to a frown switch your thoughts and feelings instantly?

Look again at Figure 14. Moving the arc and making it a straight line above the two dots creates a very different impression for me. Suddenly the mood has changed! What do you think? To me, this is still a human face, possibly one with no mouth and a heavy brow. The expression feels stern; I feel a little afraid here, gazing at this face.

Trust your words. What do you think and feel? Do you see something completely inhuman that is not a face at all? Or is it difficult to see this without seeing it as a face? It could be a plate with an uncooked spaghetti noodle on it, and two peas. What else can you get your brain and eyes to see in this image?

Subliminal Messages: Go Deep Beyond Your Threshold

All visual stimuli carry meaning, and we are either conscious of the impact they have on us, or we are not. We know it or we don't! Hidden or subliminal information exists in visual stimuli, but remains beneath our threshold of conscious knowing. Discovering what is hidden in these images is very important. Knowing how visual imagery speaks to you is empowering, because you can *process* what you want and discard what you feel will not serve you. This allows you to take control of your responses and thought patterns. You don't need to passively accept "truths" that may not benefit you; these beliefs, beneficial or otherwise, are all derived from your exposure to

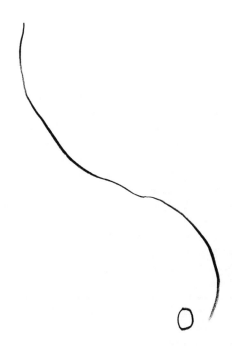

Figure 15.

Line with small oval as shut eye and teardrop.

images. In this combination of a line and oval shape, I discovered how a hidden, subliminal message took me by surprise.

Gaze at this line with a shape (Figure 15). What does it tell you? What is its destination? Often, a horizontal line going across a page suggests landscape: the horizon and a feeling of distance. For me, this line immediately feels like a landscape when I see it one way, but then I ask myself, "If this is a landscape, what is the small oval below?" It could be a small pond, an oasis in the desert, or a sinkhole. My mind tries to relate the line and shape to each other, searching for the context and content.

As I continued to gaze, the delicate undulation of this line gave me a sad feeling. The line goes downward and to the right, which to me feels like disappointment. I asked a teenager what this image meant to him, and he pointed out that the line resembled a "shut eye, and the oval is a tear." It was completely different from what I was seeing in it. He said, "Subliminally, it's a sad line and shape." That part we both felt, because I had a sad feeling while deeply gazing, but visually our impressions were very different. I was glad I asked him for his take on it. It gave me an entirely new way to see; I understood why I was feeling sad. Could it be that I saw it as a closed eye and tear, too? Unconsciously, did I feel sad despite being unaware of why the image made me feel that way?

The drawing activated unconscious memories for both of us. We knew that something deep in our minds was influenced, unleashing our emotions. Gazing at the image and discussing our impressions revealed that we could speak each others' visual-intuitive language, although we were not consciously aware of the same things until we compared our impressions.

Try It! Change Agents: Evocative Arrangements of Line and Shape

Gaze at this view of the same arrangement of line and shape (Figure 16) for a while, then show it to someone else. Let's see what happens.

Trust your words. As before, allow the image to speak to you and see what comes up. Take your time. Let it show you more than one "reading." Afterward, show it to someone else to see what they see in it! Maybe you'll discover something you didn't expect, as I did.

Drawing Conclusions

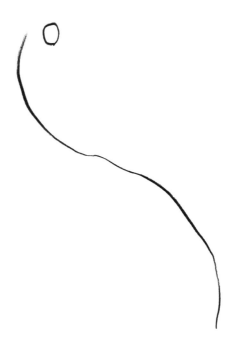

Figure 16.
Line with small oval, turned.

Gazing at these line drawings has set you on your way to developing a visual-intuitive mental library. Cultivating this kind of seeing and sensing is necessary to experience the process of visual-intuitive knowing. There are endless ways lines and shapes may occur. In stream drawings and intuitive stream drawing readings, you will need to know how to see *into* them. Beyond knowing that they convey messages, you must be able to *retrieve* those messages with your conscious mind and *feel* the emotion they hold. Because this process is both visual and intuitive, it helps you build a language of your own. That's why we're exploring what shapes and lines communicate to you. Examining these relationships will aid you as you become more intuitive. With practice, you will begin to use this vision everywhere you go. When the foundation is in place, you will be able to see everything this way. *This is a process that must be cultivated. Consciousness is a process—life is a process—living an intuitive life is a process!*

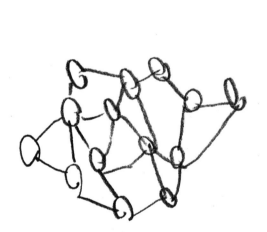

4

Drawing on the Past: Memory Drawing

Memories have a way of shadowing us. They surround us with impressions so strong that they literally hold us captive. Becoming conscious of a memory's powerful impact helps us detangle ourselves from the restrictions of the past. Without restrictions, we can be freer to create the life we would like to experience. But memories are not easy to let go of—or perhaps they do not let go of us easily. Drawing is one way to tussle with the power that memories hold over us. It lets us celebrate through creativity what we learned from our life experiences. Through stream drawing, we get into that place where both sides of the brain relax and work in concert. We express ourselves playfully and sensually, inviting feelings and impressions we've gathered over the years. Memories come out and show us what they've got. And then we get to decide what they hold for us—we exercise empowerment rather than being a victim of memories that grip us emotionally and intellectually. We come face to face with the past, and learn to use it as a guide to aid us as we grow.

Here's an example. Recently, someone told me, "If such terrible things hadn't happened to me in childhood, I believe I might have been a really great artist." My first thought was to feel very sad that she had awful early life experiences. But my second thought was that her memories (still very much alive in her) of her past might be exactly what could make her an absolutely vibrant, amazing artist! If she were to express everything she thought and felt about what happened to her, maybe she'd transform her entire life. She could use her memories to help her create forward, rather than allowing them to limit her.

Memories are loaded with emotion, which is often a great motivator for humans. All kinds of emotions from past experiences fuel our choices and put us into action. In life, we "make our marks" when we create memories; we live and learn from our experiences. Stream drawing gives us a chance to touch and create with the powerful tides of memory-based feeling within us. Consciousness arrives for us as we create. At first we may only feel relief while drawing, with nothing on our minds but enjoyment. We are who we are, and we know it. But who we perceive ourselves to be can change. Intentionally exploring how memories form our identities, our sense of self, is one way of starting anew. We have at our fingertips everything we need to activate our new way; yet, a memory may have us by the ankles, holding us in a pattern. Connecting with our deep feelings and consciously recognizing the memories they originate from may shift our sense of direction and purpose.

Memory and emotion work together. We collect memories as we live, and our impressions change as we grow. Our memories should serve us, kiss us on our way to well-being. We can even benefit from the difficult and painful ones. Severely painful memories can shape us in healthy ways or less-than-positive ways, but with work, we can be the ones to decide which it is. Once we learn what we need to from them, they don't hold much power over us. We can use them to help others who have suffered similar events. Revisiting those difficult memories as well as the easier, more pleasant ones now and then lets us see how far we've come.

Memory drawing will help you tap into a deep, intuitive source as you provide solace for yourself through emotional mark making. We do that as we stream draw— we learn to feel the flow, a good and natural sense of well-being. While drawing, we may feel our emotions in a way that is not just acceptable, but enjoyable. We stream draw and feel good, and feeling good opens up more imaginative, creative channels. Ideas and thoughts flow in and out as we express ourselves.

Your unconscious memories are potent and can offer you so much as you seek fulfillment. Stream drawing allows your unconscious and conscious mind to blend together by simply getting into the creative flow through drawing. Drawing freely, without self-criticism, gives you the ability to go inward to where many feelings and thoughts reside that you may not be aware of, and to express outward as those feelings begin to arrive in your consciousness and shifts you to new levels of inner knowing. This is an intuitive practice that enhances creativity and well-being in every way.

If we are brave enough to get creative with our memories, we learn that our unconscious mind is a storehouse for certain memories. We hold onto them without having a clue why. We also have memories we cannot forget, or get stuck on and can't let go of. This exercise will help you with both—memories you don't want to be conscious of and memories that bind you.

The process of discovery involves stream drawing while holding a specific memory in your heart and mind. You can see if new insights or perspectives become available to you. You may realize something new or be surprised when another memory emerges in connection (it may not have seemed related before). The main idea here is to make four stream drawings, each one based on a memory. You are conditioning yourself to consciously hold emotion while drawing to increase your ability to use empathic, intuitive sensing.

Are You for Real? Letting Go of Literalism

We are so trained to be literal and logical and to avoid failure (or embarrassment in class or with colleagues, and so forth) that we may *automatically try to draw a representation of a particular object while we stream draw*, even though our eyes are closed. It's as though the rational mind refuses to let us get into that stream where we do not have to be "correct." For example, in attempting to stream draw based on a happy memory, one person might think of childhood days playing baseball, close his eyes, and try to draw a baseball or other literal symbol related to his baseball memory. His drawing represents the memory in a literal or logically symbolic way, rather than drawing a meandering line that expresses the *feelings* he has when remembering this happy time. There is nothing wrong with that, especially when the objects we associate with our memories do have visual characteristics—maybe it feels great to make a round shape during stream drawing, which may look like a baseball. However, while doing this exercise, I suggest that you draw your feelings about the memory and not objects or symbols you associate with it. If you are thinking of baseballs and you draw circles over and over, that is perfectly fine. But do not be limited by the logical mind while you gain access to your emotions. This is a chance for you to engage in your feelings without restraint, and without having to prove the logic of your feelings.

Deepen Your Experience: "Draw with Emotion" and "Discover and Connect"

You have become familiar with two of the four steps used in intuitive stream drawing readings (*Gaze* and *Trust Your Words*). Now, we will practice using all four steps together: *Draw with Emotion, Gaze, Trust Your Words,* and *Discover and Connect*. First, you'll try *Drawing with Emotion* and *Discover and Connect* while stream drawing a happy memory.

Memories, as we've discussed, are full of emotional content. From powerful first impressions to beliefs wrought from routine conditioning, we carry them all. They arise often throughout the day. Many (if not all) of the emotions that we experience are a result of how we remember an event or situation. We may not even notice memories as they come and go, or take the time to assess their impact on us. Some memories protect us from danger: "I remember lightning once hit a tree I was standing near, so when I hear thunder, I take shelter in a building!" Some keep us from unfolding our wings: "I was terrible at piano lessons as a kid, and the teacher said I wasn't cut out for it; I always had a dream of playing piano, but that's impossible." We even carry the memories of the previous generations, handed down (via attitudes and expectations) to us both nonverbally and as stories. We hold tight to many of them. And they're not even ours! Some serve us well, while others are not always best for us.

It is easy to experience memories while drawing, which is enjoyable for the most part. Nobody likes to think of upsetting memories, but they're usually there, waiting for us to pull them out—if they're not lurking around to grab us out of the blue! I find that drawing about them completely relieves the stress they can bring. On the other hand, beautiful and inspirational memories send us postcards from the past, adding to our positive feelings and reminding us of our good fortune. Through stream drawing, you will see that memories are often the first thing that flow through. Since you've gazed at images, you know that they can evoke specific thoughts, feelings, associations, and meanings. You've begun a process of deepening your trust in your intuition. Drawing with emotion and using memory to generate feeling will deepen your trust and authenticate your impressions. *Discovering and connecting* while gazing at a drawing you've just created can be a spontaneous experience at times; and at others, it is a carefully cultivated process for the artist. Often, the full impact and meaning of a memory (or its connection to other memories) hits us immediately or by surprise, either while drawing or when gazing at a drawing. We take it further, exploring as many ways as possible to conceive the meaning. This is not a difficult task but a natural flow of cause and effect. If the event that created the memory is the "cause," then how we interpret the memory is the "effect."

Locating the feelings behind a memory is usually the easiest way to grab an emotion and hang onto it. Drawing while holding onto a memory is satisfying and gives you a chance to "go there" again, this time on your own terms. You never know quite where it will take you! The *Discover and Connect* phase will get you going after drawing with emotion. You will practice using your memories to connect with who you are at the present time. A particular memory may seem absolutely foreign to your current perception of your life, or connected in a remote way. Investigating that remote connection may show you a reason for how your life and identity developed in a certain way, and why.

This is a gratifying practice. You may find that you have grown a lot over time— or perhaps you will decide you've been influenced by a specific mind-set for too long and don't need it anymore. Some memories are funny—once we see how far we've come, we enjoy the way we used to be, or are proud of how we grew beyond. In other instances, we cherish what made us who we are and we seek a new way to show gratitude for our experiences and to use our new knowledge.

Drawing with Emotion

Drawing with emotion means to empathically feel while mark making. As you stream draw, you will intentionally hold an emotion, feeling it expand in your heart. Holding an emotion in your conscious mind and heart awakens intuitive sensing; drawing activates your creativity and personal will to make changes. Embrace the chance to experiment with specific emotions as you stream draw.

How Drawing with Emotion Works

You are about to have fun with this one! If you are using scrap paper, a bigger sheet can be better in these first stream drawing experiences because then you will have plenty of space to move around on the page. Take your pencil and put it into the opposite hand of the one you normally use for writing. As you relax, you will draw all around and across the page without lifting the pencil and without opening your eyes. As you did in the frozen pond exercise, draw one continuous line that meanders wherever you feel compelled to take it on the paper: up, down, or all around. Your line may form circles, zigzags, rectangles, and circles. As you draw, your hand will feel the fluctuations in pressure and gradation, pressing hard or lightly, speeding up or moving slowly across the page. You may feel compelled to use heavy pressure to make a dark line, or you may feel emotions that guide you to draw with a very light hand. Be aware while you draw of how your emotions from memory may influence you to draw slowly, quickly, lightly, or with pressure, using small or large movements.

Discover and Connect

This is the stage where we use all parts of stream drawing to gather information from our work. I call this step *Discover and Connect* because investigating a drawing's potential meaning helps us open the door to our hidden stream of consciousness. Exploring gives us a purpose and a way of making sense of it all. We can witness our experiences in a new way, acknowledge our thoughts and feelings as they flow forward, and then discover the potential in them. This is the stage of stream drawing that shows us our purpose and potential.

How Discover and Connect Works

Once you get comfortable trusting your words as they arrive into your conscious mind, you will find that you develop a quiet sense of empathic, intuitive knowing. While absorbing an image with a sense of gratitude and ease, you will experience a feeling of enchantment so pleasant that you may feel yourself light up from head to toe. This wonderment is the sign that you are activating your "higher self," your spirit within. This aspect of self is your total sense of well-being that resides within you *perpetually*. Life's complications may block our awareness of it, but it is always there. This is the aspect of you that is already complete, enriched, and open to your heart's consciousness. Stream drawing and gazing allow you to unblock and feel the deep beauty that is a natural state at the core of your being. The discover and connect step takes you to a meditative state where you can get a real understanding of your experiences and impressions. Discover and connect with expectant openness and see what begins to make sense.

Try It! Create Your Own Memory Drawing

Sit comfortably and take a long look at the blank paper before you. Breathe in the expansive, untouched possibilities that it represents. Take your pencil in your non-dominant hand. Holding your hand in a relaxed way over the paper, softly touch your pencil on the paper and close your eyes. Think of a childhood memory that makes you happy. For many people, the first thing that comes to mind when searching for a happy memory is all the hard or sad ones! They jump into our minds and hearts more easily for some reason, shouting for our attention. Let them arrive in your mind and heart and then let them leave you like a butterfly for now. If you are short on happy childhood memories, think of a recent memory that gives you joy, or a wish or an ideal instead.

Settle in and sense a time when you were young—when any event, person, place, or thing made you feel good, whether it was small or large. As you draw, eyes closed, think of this happy memory. Allow your pencil to go wherever your hand takes it. Allow your pencil to glide in one continuous line. Without lifting the pencil off the paper, go all over the page, varying pressure as you draw. With happiness, let your hand make marks freely. You may make swirls and spirals or lines and random shapes—whatever you feel like drawing. Sense the emotions that guide your hand.

You may wish to draw for a few minutes or for only several seconds. As the pencil moves along the surface of the paper, it is an instrument of your thoughts and emotions. Draw as you feel the memory of that happiness move across your heart and mind. Stop drawing when you are finished.

An Example of a Happy Memory Drawing

Figure 17 shows a happy memory stream drawing made by a twelve-year-old girl named Brianna. This sample is not shown to give the impression that your drawing should be like hers. Yours may look very different, and it should! No two memory drawings will ever look exactly alike. There is no right way or wrong way. I am sharing it here (as well as other samples in the book) so you can see how stream drawing can evolve. I hope that seeing some drawings may inspire you as you create your own.

Brianna Drew with Emotion: Brianna sat down with a blank piece of paper and a pencil and called up a happy memory. She closed her eyes and held the memory in her mind as she drew. She let the pencil roam all over the page. When she was finished, she opened her eyes and told me her happy memory was of a time when she was quite a bit younger and found a twenty dollar bill on the playground.

Brianna Gazed: To Brianna's surprise, when she opened her eyes and gazed at the drawing, she saw in the middle a twenty dollar bill. In the center of the drawing, you

Happy Memory Drawing

twenty dollar bill

"I Felt the ocean"

Figure 17.
Brianna's happy memory drawing.

might see a large rectangular shape reminiscent of a dollar bill, with a number two in the center.

Brianna created the shape of the twenty dollar bill while closing her eyes and doing her happy memory drawing. Again, it is a natural impulse to try to depict a literal representation of a memory, rather than simply holding the feelings of the memory while drawing with eyes closed. But in this case, it did not inhibit Brianna from getting into the flow for her stream drawing. Many drawings surprise us. Although she did not think she was trying to be literal, Brianna was surprised to see what to her resembled a twenty dollar bill in the center of her happy memory drawing. She drew her happy memory truly *feeling the emotion* of happiness.

Brianna's reaction was to intuitively, spontaneously turn the drawing around to see it in four different ways. She marveled at the shapes, lines, and multiple views of each. We will talk about this part of the process later; for now, know that while gazing, it's okay to turn the drawing around to see what a new perspective says to you.

Brianna Trusted Her Words: After Brianna completed the drawing, opened her eyes, and saw the twenty dollar bill in the center, she said that what came to mind as she drew was the "feeling of the ocean."

Brianna Discovered and Connected: Brianna's "feeling of the ocean" was not logically connected to her memory of finding the twenty dollar bill. The association took her by surprise. She said the ocean came into her mind because that was another happy memory from her childhood: swimming and playing with her brother. *Drawing while feeling that happiness* unexpectedly brought her the memory of other happy times, splashing in the ocean! Brianna's emotional intelligence delivered more happiness when she gazed at her drawing—all in a matter of moments.

Try It! Happy Memory Drawing

Bring up a memory of something that made you happy from any point in your life. Focus on capturing the feeling of happiness as best you can. You need to be comfortable so your thoughts and feelings can flow. As you deepen your breathing, ask your higher self to bring you a happy memory.

Draw with Emotion (as described on page 56): When you feel relaxed and calm, close your eyes. Let a happy memory rise to the surface. Maybe you see it like a movie in your mind, or you remember specific details. Try to capture the feelings you had during that happy event in your life, and when you feel that happiness, keep it with you for as long as you can. It may slip away for a moment (or get interrupted), but allow any passing thoughts to drift out of your mind like a soft wind blowing. Focus on the happy memory. With that feeling stirring your heart, open your eyes to place your pencil on the paper. Then, close your eyes again and draw using your nondominant hand. Continue to see the memory in your mind and hold your happiness as you draw.

Gaze: Gaze at your stream drawing in a gentle, appreciative way. Take in the marks you made and let them just "be" on the paper. Gradually, let your eyes wander around. Gaze at different areas of the drawing with an open heart. Your happy memory may still cling to you, or it may slip away as you explore the stream drawing. Either way, it does not matter. Other, unexpected memories may surface, and if they do, enjoy them. Gaze and accept whatever comes to you.

You may notice your eyes are drawn to specific shapes, lines, or negative space. You may want to turn the drawing upside down or sideways.

Gazing has two parts: using your physical eyes and seeing with your intuitive intelligence. You are beginning to use your third eye, another kind of vision—the seeing you do without your actual eyes, such as when you picture something in your mind, experience a memory, or dream. When you gaze without an agenda, your intuition arises. Your unconscious mind may show you what it perceives in the drawing, such as a sign, symbol, or shape that is reminiscent of a familiar object.

Do not judge your drawing, just enjoy it. You took nothing—a piece of blank paper—and turned it into *something*. Your creative willpower is coming into play!

Trust Your Words: Now, while gazing at your happy memory drawing, notice if any words come to mind. Is there a word to express how you felt while you were drawing? If a word surfaces, write it down. It may not be logical or even seem to relate to the memory but trust it anyway.

As you observe your happy memory stream drawing, notice the shape and character of the lines, the gradation, and the way the whole drawing looks. Write as the words come to you. Don't worry about making a logical connection. If no words appear, simply enjoy the visual attitude of the drawing (the expression in the line) and simply describe what you see. You may write "angular," "circular," or "wiry." Just describe the basics. As you write, take note of any thoughts or emotions that arrive. Remember not to place a value judgment on the drawing. You are describing the qualities of the drawing, not its worthiness. Your drawings represent an intuitive process, and are not meant to be subject to critique.

Discover and Connect: Embrace all you have done so far. You drew while holding the feelings of a happy memory, and gazed at it. You trusted your words as they came while gazing at this drawing. Now you get to dig around for the treasure in your drawing by finding ways in which the memory, images, and words all connect. At first, they may not seem to, but you may make playful discoveries while seeking the connections. How does your happy memory relate to the imagery you saw while gazing? What words came to mind when you trusted that the ones you needed would arrive? If nothing connects for you, put the drawing aside and come back to it a little later. You can revisit a stream drawing anytime to see if there is gold in it for you. Being easygoing and playful helps, I find, more than being too serious. When I'm playful, I am more likely to recognize connections than if I'm locked into a certain idea about something.

Try It! Angry Memory Drawing

Draw with Emotion: Turn the paper over, and this time think of something that makes you angry. I'm not trying to ruin your day! In fact, thinking of an angry feeling while drawing might help you. Humans process anger (especially repressed anger) without being aware of it. Drawing the feeling allows you to acknowledge your anger as it takes form on paper. This is very powerful, especially if you express it in a creative, purposeful way that is not harmful or destructive. Drawing is an excellent way to bring up our unconscious feelings. You may not want to dredge up your anger; those feelings can be overwhelming and make you feel out of control. Yet, too often we shove our emotions inward or ignore them, and this can lead to distress, illness, and dis-ease. Just because we deny our feelings does not mean they are not there.

Anger lets you know what you do not want in life. It helps you identify what situations or circumstances are not good for you. Anger can motivate you to make change—a positive effect. Take a deep breath and honor that emotion within you.

Engaging with your anger and working with it creatively is an excellent way to process your emotional response.

In thinking of an angry emotion, you might remember something from childhood again, or something you are dealing with now. You might remember a person who did something you think wasn't right or fair, or it might be a situation that you have not overcome. The angry memory might be anger at yourself or at things that are wrong in the world. Whatever it is, you must fully capture your emotion so that you can feel its undeniable power. Allow the feelings of anger to surface as you ready your pencil and paper. Once again put your pencil on the paper using your nondominant hand, close your eyes, and draw while you feel this anger. Work until you are finished—you'll know when you want to stop.

Gaze: As you open your eyes to gaze at this angry memory drawing, notice how it feels to look at the image you created. Compare your happy memory drawing with this angry memory drawing, side by side. How did drawing while feeling an angry emotion differ from drawing while feeling a happy one? How are the lines and shapes different? Did your hand press harder during the joyful drawing or the angry drawing? Did you draw slower or faster?

Trust Your Words: Look at the drawing from the angry memory. If any words come to mind about how the image looks or makes you feel, write them down. Remember, they may have nothing at all to do with your memory, or even seem logical. Trust whatever words come to your mind. I don't care if the words are "scrub brush" or "apple pie"—just go with it!

Spend a few moments looking at both drawings. When you are finished comparing them, get more paper. Let's do a few more memory drawings. If it feels uncomfortable to do more drawings, take a walk or do something else. We'll come back when it feels good to call up new memories.

Discover and Connect: Anger is one of those emotions that finds its way into many areas of our lives, often without our awareness. Making connections and discovering those memories in a new light can be real change agents for us, deepening our intuitive process. An angry memory may be about something very specific, and we would like to think it stays in a place in our minds where we have it under complete control. Yet, once we begin to gaze and draw with emotion, we connect to anger in a new way. In the *Discover and Connect* phase of this intuitive process, we make images that give us a deeper sense of our anger. Your angry stream drawing may connect with a situation unrelated to the one you concentrated on during the drawing. How are the two events similar to each other? Does all anger feel the same?

You may feel during *discover and connect* that some anger is easy to let go of. Images in your stream drawing will potentially trigger times when you felt anger and coped well, releasing it. Use the stream drawing to help you feel anger and appreciate the emotion for all the power in it, no matter how unpleasant. Then, get new insights into how you can transform the anger into constructive action. Write down any images you see in the drawing, even if they don't make sense right away. Contemplate them. Relate to those images and find the meaning in them. Take your time!

Try It! Sad Memory Drawing

Draw with Emotion: Sit calmly and breathe softly, pencil and paper ready. You might want to close your eyes to see what sad memory will surface. Often, sad memories or events in which we got hurt are the first memories to arise in the conscious mind. Sadness is one of the emotions all humans experience. We also can find it hard to let go of sadness. I can think of something that made me sad ages ago, and in a snap, I feel the same deep, concave feeling in my chest, as though no time has passed.

As you ask for a sad memory to visit your consciousness, you may find that a personal one does not surface. Instead, you may get a macrocosm or "big picture" memory, such as the state of the economy, damaging natural disasters, or wars raging around the world. Don't stress about retrieving a particular memory, just allow what comes to float into your heart and mind.

Once you have a sad memory, allow yourself to sit with it for a bit. You may even feel sensations in your body, your stomach or throat. Emotional energy stirs up your physical being, so noticing the way your body takes in memories is important. (You will see how much it connects to conscious awareness and intuitive knowing when you begin doing intuitive stream drawing readings.) It may not be comfortable to feel the sad feelings again—who needs that, right?—or to be aware of the places in your body where emotions churn, but being in touch with sadness will help you draw it out for a constructive purpose. You can shift some of your emotions once you start creating. Identifying where sadness or other emotions are most active in your body will also help you consciously draw them out into awareness, therefore releasing them gradually onto paper.

Close your eyes to draw when you are ready. As you've done before, draw while feeling and remembering what makes you sad, or what made you sad long ago. Draw however it feels good to draw. Does it feel good to go fast or slow? Would you like to press hard, lightly, or vary your stroke? Using your nondominant hand, create one continuous line that may turn and twist into shapes, peaks, and valleys. The feeling may surface as though it just occurred, even though you may have experienced this sad event decades ago. Draw with your eyes closed until you are ready to stop moving the pencil and open your eyes.

Gaze: Now, gaze at the drawing you made. Allow your feelings to adjust. Your eyes may wander on the page or focus on the picture as a whole. Relax as you gaze at this image. What thoughts or feelings come to mind? Do you still feel sad, or even a little angry at having to hold a sad memory in your conscious mind? Do you have any sad memories that you carry around in your mind (or have regular inward conversations about)? Allow your sadness to build or subside as you gaze. Gazing with an open, expectant, accepting attitude will help you as your emotions fluctuate. Notice what shapes jump out at you and how they may speak to you. Do you recognize any images that might appear at random, much the way we see bunnies or cotton candy shapes in clouds? Do any of the images surprise you? Connect images that don't logically relate (or never occurred to you before now) to your sad memory. (For example, in a radio interview I did, a caller said she had diabetes. I quickly did a stream drawing where a rabbit was clearly visible—though of course I did the drawing with my eyes closed, focusing on her diabetes. I could connect her diabetes to fear, since for me, personally "rabbit" has come to represent getting over fears). Gaze at and enjoy the drawing for what it is. Look and let the feeling of the drawing work on your mind and heart.

Trust Your Words: As you gazed at the stream drawing you created, did any words come to mind? Any names or particular feelings? Often, our feelings bring up words that describe them. I suggest writing notes away from the drawing area so you can concentrate on the visual imagery and keep the drawing area uncomplicated by handwriting for now. Write the words (and trust them).

Discover and Connect: Sad memory stream drawings may feel similar to angry memory drawings. The feelings still grip us, even years later. Discovering and connecting requires that we really be open to whatever image we see in the stream drawing, even if it seems impossible.

Don't think too hard. Just take in the imagery, make a note of each thing you see, and any thoughts or associations that the images bring up for you. If a general feeling of sadness hangs with you during the *Discover and Connect* phase, don't try to push it away. Just record what comes to you without judgment. Discovering how sadness has played a part in your life, through your disposition or in your life experiences, can empower you, because once you get a view of sadness's effect on your life, you can create with it, and not just be subject to it. One sad event may not seem to relate to another, yet you may realize there are connections in the form of repeated patterns, themes, and circumstances you no longer need. Knowing this can help you move forward anew. Discover and connect with your strength and resolve. Let your stream drawing show you the way!

 ## Try It! Nervous Memory Drawing

Draw with Emotion: Have you ever felt nervous? Maybe you felt that way on the first day of school, before giving a speech, seeing someone you had a crush on, or in the presence of your boss. This time we will go inward and connect to the anxieties that talk to us all day long. So often we are so on-task in our lives, performing duties or fulfilling responsibilities, that we do not pay attention to our nerves.

Breathe in deeply as you sit with your pencil and paper ready (again using your nondominant hand). Allow a memory of nervousness to surface. There may be more than one, so settle in and see which nervous memory demands your attention at this moment. When you are ready, close your eyes and draw while sensing how it felt to be nervous. Let your pencil roam as your hand channels the feelings of nervousness, through your arm and onto the paper. When you are ready, put the pencil down and open your eyes.

Gaze: Breathe in deeply as you gaze at the drawing you made. Take it all in: the periphery, the center, and the areas that most grab your attention. Enjoy the marks you made. Feel gratitude for being able to express your emotion through pencil and paper. Notice how you felt while you were drawing, and how you feel now that you're done. Do you still feel nervous? Has the memory faded, or does the drawing keep the feeling of anxiety alive in you? How does this nervous memory drawing compare to your happy or angry memory drawings? Does it have anything in common with your sad memory drawing?

Trust Your Words: Notice any words that materialized as you gazed at your drawing. Trust what comes to mind, and write it down on the paper away from your drawing. You might find that you felt a certain way while drawing, which brought up a certain word; gazing may evoke completely different feelings and words. Make note of that, if you like.

Discover and Connect: Nervous memories sometimes have an abstract quality to them. We can remember the specific events that made us nervous, and also recall long periods of time when we felt a generalized nervousness that is hard to describe. Nervous stream drawings give you the opportunity to adjust to and work with nervousness. All kinds of random images may appear in your drawing, or you may feel waves of emotion; you may not have a logical explanation for any of it. You may get a feeling of dread or of elation while gazing at the drawing and not be able to explain why right away. During discovering and connecting, the images and emotions do not have to immediately make sense, but trust what comes so that you can find new ways to look at nervousness. Take special note of anything you feel while gazing at your nervous memory drawing. It may hold signals for you. You may appreciate old emotions or let go of ones you decide you no longer need to nurture. Either way, work with patience to connect with a sense of respect for the experiences you've encountered that have given you this emotion.

Try It! Put It All Together

Once you have made happy, angry, sad, and nervous memory drawings, spread them all out and look at them together. Do not judge or criticize them. Quietly observe the marks you made. If any words or thoughts come to mind as you compare one drawing with another, you may want to write them down. Your impressions are important. Observe your drawings with appreciation and ask yourself these questions:

- Does the happy memory drawing look similar to the nervous memory drawing?
- Does the angry memory drawing stand out from the others? If so, why?
- Does one drawing have heavier or lighter lines than the others?
- Which drawing gripped me emotionally the most in each phase: stream drawing, gazing, trusting my words, and discovering and connecting?

Try to locate imagery in each memory drawing that may connect you directly with the emotion you held while drawing. Do other memories pop into your awareness? If so, notice them. What made them arrive? Was it the way a line created a shape? Or is it something that you cannot explain logically? Use these memory drawings, assemble them, and see their differences and similarities to help you gain visual-intuitive information.

Put your drawings aside when you are finished. You can take them out later or another day to see if new insights or images pop up. If you see a shape that reminds you of an animal, for example, take note. It might become a meaningful symbol to you in relation to that particular memory or the emotions associated with it. As I mentioned earlier, I see a rabbit in some of my intuitive stream drawing readings. Rabbits have come to represent abundance on one hand and fears on the other—fears I need to get over. This evolved when a rabbit shape appeared in my sad memory drawing, prompting me to ask, "What does 'rabbit' mean to me?" Keep asking yourself questions while *discovering and connecting* each memory drawing. Savor the characteristics in each one as reflections of your higher self and capacity for emotional, intuitive expansion.

Drawing Conclusions

You have experimented with the way memory and perception work together to give you a full range of emotions, and you've seen how stream drawing can help call up the emotions connected to memory. Through the exercises in this book, you've discovered that drawing, an act of expression, is a harmonious, natural way to process emotions. You've taken that one step further by seeing what the stream drawing offers after it is created; you've developed your visual-intuitive language through line, shape, texture, and form. Gazing at all four memory stream drawings adds another dimension.

Trusting your words and making discoveries give you a new perspective on what you once experienced. Memory drawings show you how to get creative, using the memories as a source of strength and healing potential. Making connections gives you another way to glean gold from even the hard memories: they are *yours*. You have the creative willpower to use them for growth and to gain clarity, using them to your benefit as you move into the future.

Next, we'll explore emotions in new ways as we continue to develop that language.

5

Drawing Out Emotion: Empathic Curiosity and Imaginative Interplay

You have done stream drawings using memories to activate emotional responses to begin developing a visual-intuitive language all your own. Experimenting more with emotions and seeing how they activate our creative, intuitive responses will further expand your new way of communicating. Allowing yourself time to get playful with emotion, using your imagination and a sense of curiosity, is what gives you creative potency while feeling and sensing.

The connection between emotion and imagination is interesting because once we have a feeling, we want to express it. We may search all our lives to find the best way of expressing that feeling. Thoughts, too, seek ideal forms of expression and imagination and can help you demonstrate your thinking through a creative process. It's important to stay curious and be flexible as you learn more; it will help you understand better, experience new perspectives, and enjoy a feeling of freedom. Your life will gain momentum as you move closer to the source that describes the true essence within.

Your imagination is your creative, intuitive playscape. Think of it as a place within you where your curiosity is boundless. You need to go there and enjoy your perceptions as much as possible. When you enter the realm of your imagination, you

71

go to the place where you are most open and receptive. There, you receive ideas out of the blue. This is the place where as you grow in life; your perceptions change as you mature. Since this state of playfulness or openness is where intuitive information enters our consciousness, we need to pay attention to it. By being creative and expressive, we allow the imaginative forces within to start their magic.

Stream drawing, because of its creative and emotional power, can take us to that intuitive-creative place within (especially when we draw with genuine emotion). Emotion is a strong motivator for expression and for seeking answers. Sometimes we want relief from our strong emotion, or we feel we'll burst if we don't act on our inspiration. We find that we are able to discover new impressions and so we are constantly accumulating new information.

Creativity and imagination help generate a sense of rebirth in our emotional lives. When we let emotion and imagination work together, we literally shift reality. We bring ideas into our hands out of thin air. Every idea starts in the realm of the imagination; when we're creative with our emotions, something comes into form. Those surprises are known as "happy accidents" in the art world. We are bringing out what is not concrete (and so, we think, not "real"). Bringing thoughts, feelings, and desires into being by expressing them into reality is where the big shift occurs.

The force of emotion can be overpowering at times. Your physical response to it may be immediate. Emotion engages the body, and the urge to act on it is instinctual. Think of being steaming angry, feeling rage roll through your body, temples, and throat. You might clench your fist, make a growling sound, or kick out. If you were to kick an object in an attempt to release the anger, you'd feel the effects. Artful, intuitive, and creative expression offers a way to take on emotions—even the difficult ones, like anger—and constructively reassemble them to communicate in a concrete, healing, and re-envisioning way. We see emotions in a new context, with a new perspective. The emotion begins to be a thing we experienced (past). Our new creation represents a step forward (future). A new sense of self-acceptance is formed.

While drawing, which is an act of intention, your unconscious mind works in harmony with your conscious one to process the feelings you've gathered in your lifetime. You have engaged in this interplay and felt firsthand how memory brings up emotion. The emotive and sensual experience of drawing is a good outlet for those emotions because it is mentally, physically, and emotionally harmonious. Being in harmony supports well-being, which means we are able to take responsibility for our actions and choose the life we would most like to experience. "Drawing out" emotions is a good thing.

We have explored one way—using our memories as conduits—that drawing connects us to our emotions and intuitive sensing. As you've seen in the previous chapters, drawing allows you to experience and express emotions all at once. The process of making marks is action oriented, sensual and emotive. Drawing shifts our awareness into a place that unlocks personal unconscious memory and allows us to coast and to "be" with our emotions while gaining awareness of them. We begin to feel—and we're okay with it. We draw and we feel good doing it, and in that state of good feeling something more happens. Creativity gains momentum, as a sense of curiosity and self-expression expounds upon a physical relationship to emotional force. We can take charge of our lives. If we never became aware, we'd just be reacting without knowing why. Through drawing, we open to our imagination and release tension. It is probably one of the most powerful practices we have.

The more conscious we are of our thoughts and feelings, the more we understand ourselves, our motives, and our uniqueness. No two people are exactly alike on this earth; individuality is our true heritage to share. But how can we share it when we aren't even sure of what it is, or if we have barriers up that block us from making our mark in the world? How can we realize our potential if we are not sure what it is in the first place?

We are born and begin sensing right away. We form impressions that hold significance for us. As we develop, we are conditioned by our surroundings and the culture we live in. We take on responsibilities: our first responsibility is to our well-being and emotional health. The stronger and better we are in terms of working with our emotions, the easier it is to live. We have a better chance to create the life situations we'd like to experience if we explore within, while expressing outwardly through practices like drawing.

One Continuous Line: Keep the Feeling Flowing

It is just too easy for an inner voice to stop you in your tracks while you're trying to get into the flow. Mental obstacles interfere with that process, which relies on opening and accepting. When you stream draw, you do not have to make decisions or consider space and form, two things that might interrupt your flow. The idea is that *once your pencil and paper have contact, the flow begins.* Picking up the pencil can cause a break in the flow, and you do not want that. Once you know how to get into your blissful flow, without blocking yourself, you can create in any way, at any time you like!

Your continuous line wants to go in all kinds of directions. It may loop and twist, get wiry, slope downward, or shoot upward. It's producing dynamic and detailed visual-intuitive relationships. Yes, one line can do that! In my current practice of doing intuitive stream drawing readings, I use the same single continuous line method to get me into an intuitive zone. My drawings become complex enough to offer volumes of meaning. Each intuitive stream drawing reading is like a dream, offering more the longer you gaze at it.

So as you stream draw, that one meandering line will get complicated very quickly when you gaze at it. You'll see a visual feast of line, shape, and form (including negative space). The thing you thought was so simple—it felt simple when you were drawing!—has transformed.

With practice, you will stream draw with your eyes open. You will know how to get in that intuitive zone and stay in it all day. Your creativity will overflow, unrestricted! You'll also begin to create your own techniques, exploring methods of expanding your sixth sense.

 Try It! Stream Draw with Emotion

First, you will need a pencil and paper. The bigger the sheet, the better! If you can get a large newsprint pad and put it on the table in front of you, that will be ideal. That way, you can really stretch out your arms while you generate that good feeling that comes from stream drawing with emotion.

Think of a word describing a feeling or an attitude and write it at the top of your paper. Below is a list to choose from, or you may come up with your own. You'll use this emotion to do a line stream drawing, followed by stream drawings with lines, shapes, and marks together.

Controlling	Frightened		Pessimistic
Determined	Furious		Tired
Ethereal	Optimistic		Weary
Excited	Pained		Wise
	Passive		

Once you've chosen a word, sit down and get comfortable, with your paper ready and your pencil in your nondominant hand. Close your eyes and breathe deeply as you meditate on the meaning of the word. Consider any life experiences you might associate with this word. You may at first think of a literal meaning, but don't stop there. Go deeper, and capture your personal meaning.

Draw with Emotion: As you concentrate on the word with your eyes closed, you may find that you are thinking of its definition. Certain associations may occur to you, such as a particular person, pet, or event. A seemingly unrelated memory or scene may float into your mind's eye. Take note of these thoughts. Allow them to arrive safely in your conscious mind. When you are ready to draw, make one line on the paper. As you did in the frozen pond exercise, draw without stopping or lifting the pencil. Your line may be long and flowing, with swirls and circles, or rigid and fierce. It may be a short, stubby line. It doesn't need to be logical; it is how *you* interpret the feeling of your word.

Gaze: When you are finished, open your eyes. Remember that "to gaze" means "to behold with an open and appreciative countenance." Enjoy the marks you created. Observe the line's shape and general expression. Note its gradation. Is it dark, faint, or both? Is it sinuous or full of right angles? Does it look the way you imagined it would while you made it? Gaze and let your eyes absorb the imagery. You will begin to process your drawing consciously as you take your time gazing.

Trust Your Words: As you gaze, some memories, associations, and words will come into your consciousness. Keep listening for them as you gaze, and jot down the thoughts that arrive—follow each thread, even if it is not logical, or if it brings up entirely different memories than you thought it would. Trust your words fully.

Discover and Connect: This is the moment to unite your observations of your drawing's character with its content. Exploring its meanings, you trusted your words. Now, discover why certain ideas came to mind when gazing. Write anything down that helps describe why lines and shapes conjure up specific memories and associations with the particular emotion you chose.

An Example of Stream Drawing with Emotion

I Drew with Emotion: For my stream drawing in Figure 18, I chose the word "passive." I concentrated on how I feel about that word and invited memories to stream into my mind's eye and my heart. While preparing to draw—closing my eyes and taking a deep breath—I kept seeing a tunnel. This annoyed me at first, so I resisted it. No other mental images came to me about the word passive. I got frustrated, because no matter what, the tunnel image remained in my mind's eye. I held the emotion that came with the word passive and began stream drawing. I did not draw the tunnel image that came into (and would not leave) my mind, but instead held the feelings of "passive" in my mind and heart. My hand felt weak as I held the pencil.

Once I stopped resisting the image of a tunnel, I let myself think about why it came to mind. I realized a tunnel is an underpass, and that really connected me to what it feels like when I am passive or when I perceive someone else as passive. When I looked at the times I had been passive, I saw that I was resisting conflict, or wishing not to hurt someone else's feelings. I remembered holding back over the

Figure 18.
Passive line.

years and not voicing what I wanted to say. I was "passing under" a situation or argument. This is not always courageous or healthy. Sometimes, especially when I was younger, I just wanted to be liked, or tried to avoid a big debate. Even when I had a lot to say, I declined out of a lack of confidence, perhaps, or because I focused more on how I perceived the other person to be feeling.

When I understood why the tunnel came into mind, I was ready for the next step. I kept my eyes closed and drew a line on the paper in front of me. I noticed while holding "passive," I felt very little tension and pressed lightly on the paper. My hand guided me to make a pale mark on the paper.

I Gazed: Gazing at what I had drawn, I saw a weak kind of up-sweeping line, with changes in gradation going from an even pressure to an almost invisible pressure and back again to an even pressure. The line also had a loop that looked like a teardrop to me. I realized that I sometimes feel annoyed with myself or others for being passive. Seeing the teardrop, though, gave me another way of looking at the word passive. I began to write my thoughts on the paper, under the line. More impressions flooded in.

I Trusted My Words: Words and thoughts came easily with this one and I jotted them down (Figure 19). I wrote that maybe passivity comes from a deep sadness (represented to me by the teardrop image). If so, sadness could affect the way someone handles difficult situations. The will to assert oneself or resist may wane when a person carries sadness. Perhaps my feelings about my own passivity made me sad. Maybe I could take risks and respond with integrity instead.

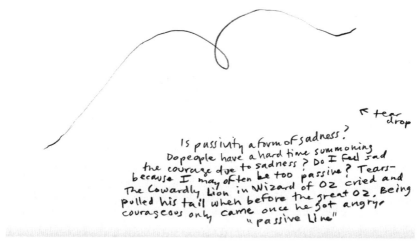

Figure 19.
Passive line with my notations.

I also wondered how the word "courage" relates to the word "passive." This instantly reminded me of the Cowardly Lion from *The Wizard of Oz*. He was in tears before the Great Oz. He pulled his own tail, trying to summon up his courage. However, he did not actually get assertive until later in the film when he became angry. Was courage dependent on anger? Did it represent the threshold of patience? At first, the lion ran away from the wizard. But later, when he realized the wizard was a mere mortal, the lion became brave and resolute. My stream drawing line showed me that courage may derive from anger or indignation, which fuels someone to rise

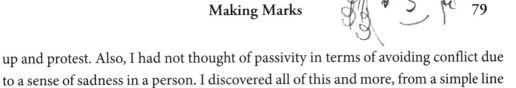

up and protest. Also, I had not thought of passivity in terms of avoiding conflict due to a sense of sadness in a person. I discovered all of this and more, from a simple line drawing!

Furthermore, I added to my discovery because the more I looked at this line shaped like a teardrop, the more I saw other things in it. I saw a handlebar mustache, which makes me remember a pizza place I used to go to where they showed endless loop films (the word "loop" here connects to my description of the teardrop—an interesting synchronistic connection). The films were of mustachioed men from the 1920s, barbershop quartets wearing striped shirts. If I really go back to that memory, I was just beginning to work with being "passive" versus "assertive" back then. I was a teenager learning to become an individual. I often wanted to have my say, but let myself down by being too passive. I don't particularly like this memory, and the old films depress me in retrospect—but there it is, all the same.

The other thing that occurred to me was that if I looked at this drawing one way, it could resemble femininity. The curvaceous line looked like a feminine bust or cleavage. So I followed that line of thought and put the idea of women with the word femininity. Women were always conditioned to be passive or to say things very lightly, I thought. Growing up in the South, I remember once saying something forthright, and an older man told me, "You are being ugly!" He did not like my assertive tone. It hurt my feelings, but I decided he was wrong to put a value judgment on my opinion—he labeled me as ugly for speaking out, confusing feminine beauty with assertiveness as a way to control or undermine me. With this memory in mind, I decided to revisit times when I deferred to social conditioning as a result of my culture and gender.

All of this content from a single little line with a loop in it!

Examining your memories and associations might seem like an exercise in self-involvement. But I assure you that it is *not* a waste of time. Being in touch with your unconscious memories and associations can help you use your intuition in your daily life in ways that will improve your life and others' as well.

Notable Impressions:
Journaling the Insights Your Stream Drawings Give You

You can see that as I trusted my words while gazing at this stream drawing of a line based on the word "passive." Thoughts and feelings easily streamed in from my life experiences and impressions. Meanings began to occur to me that I had not considered before.

As you get comfortable with intuitive exploration, you may consider switching from loose-leaf paper or newsprint to a blank sketchbook. It will help you keep track of your stream line drawings and notations. You will build intimacy with yourself and boost your intuitive intelligence, as your unconscious and conscious mind work together. Later, when you do a stream drawing for the purpose of solving a problem, some familiar line characteristics will signal meanings to you! For example, the teardrop shape signifies more to me than it once did. If I see a looping line with a teardrop (these often show up in intuitive stream drawings I do to help my clients), then I know it indicates more than a sad experience. I can communicate with clients more meaningfully, because passivity is connected to sadness, which is an opportunity for courage. Courage may come when we get angry, but it arrives when we need to assert our integrity. The starting point is understanding that sadness may hold us back from voicing our opinion. Instead, we choose passivity. Once we understand what that sadness is, we can heal it. We feel more confident when sharing an opinion, and assert our boundaries. We become free.

This is an example of how much guidance and rich content you can derive from a single, simple line. I hope this gives you an idea of the great potential this process has for you, as you build an intuitive language all your own. Repeating this exercise with other emotions will add new images to explore on paper. Connecting what comes into your mind and heart before, during, and after the stream drawing will help you identify the meanings according to your own experiences, and as you create more and more stream drawings, familiar images may come through, in addition to new ones.

Do More Stream Drawing!

Using your emotions and personal experiences, continue to practice stream drawing with your nondominant hand. Allow your pencil to roam freely over the page as you express what you feel. Your line may make shapes or even "interrupted" marks, such as dashes and dots. Go with your natural inclinations. Remember to breathe deeply and stay relaxed. Keep your eyes closed, if it helps you maintain your flow. Follow the steps we've practiced:

> Draw with Emotion
> Gaze
> Trust Your Words
> Discover and Connect

Try doing more than one stream drawing so you can experience the variation in how they feel and what they look like. You might try this with two very different emotions: one stream drawing might be "love," while the other is "hate." Do they feel different while you create them? Put them side by side while you gaze. See how they play off of each other. Comparing two stream drawings is another way to enjoy and deepen your perceptions; of course, you're also sharpening your visual-intuitive language. It will give you new insight into the potency of your emotions as expressed through line, shape, and texture.

Drawing Conclusions

In this chapter, you've found that almost any emotion can be accessed and expressed while stream drawing. You may also have noticed that you can stream draw and not feel anything but good while you do it. This chapter gave you a chance to try making stream drawings of more than one emotion, and then gazing to consider their characteristics. What did you discover? Do your stream drawings look and feel alike, or are there specific marks that show how your emotions differ? Was there a power in discovering connections and similarities or contrasts in your emotion-based stream drawings? In the next chapter, we'll explore other ways to find connections and receive messages through streaming in the flow.

6

Streaming and Dreaming: The Link between Dreams and Intuition

Dreams connect us to our creative, imaginative, and unconscious brilliance—and so does stream drawing, much in the same way.

Dreams are visual teachers. Drawings are, too; responding to art is a subjective, visual process—they teach us through visual language. Drawings, like dreams, provide us with an opportunity to get in touch with what drives us. Dreams are journeys into the unconscious mind, and we create stream drawings to get into an unconscious flow while we're awake. Stream drawings are rich with messages that arrive in the same way that dream information is delivered.

When we fall asleep and dream, our minds open to our intuitive universe, full of emotion and knowledge. Though we cannot see with our physical eyes, we have another kind of vision—that of the unconscious, the creative, the spiritual, and intuitive.

As I learned to cope with intuitive feelings and information in my dreams, I forged better ways to understand them and work with them. Dreams have taught me all my life, from childhood days when I felt completely swamped by their emotional, psychological, and visually graphic content, to my dreams today. As a child they weighed on me heavily; the cinematic images would follow me all day. They became a psychological burden for me. In high school, I finally decided to start working with my dreams. Rather than feeling overwhelmed, I wanted to actively participate. I learned to interact with my dreams so that I could experience the ones I really wanted (such as flying dreams!) and do something about the upsetting ones. I learned to handle a troubling dream by either stopping it midstream or by journaling about it, using its power to my advantage.

If you'd like to participate with dream messages but do not remember your dreams, there are many things you can do to help yourself remember them. Later in this chapter, we'll explore some ways to train the conscious mind to cooperate with the unconscious mind through remembering dreams.

The Power of Dreams

Dreams have the power to send very big messages, even if we don't understand them right away. Most people remember at least one influential dream they've had—maybe from childhood, maybe a scary or bad one. I remember a bad dream that was a turning point for me. At a very young age, I had a tremendously disturbing dream about my parents. It shattered me. When I woke up, my parents were entertaining friends after dinner. I could not go back to sleep or stay in bed, so I tiptoed out into the den. My dad was making drinks called "grasshoppers," rich green with foamy cream on top. (This was the 1960s. My parents were still relatively young, and this drink was kind of a fad at the time.) I stood beside my dad as he stirred the drinks, feeling terrible dread about my dream. He asked me what I was doing up. With a panicked feeling, I told him, "I had a bad dream." He was easygoing with me and asked me about my dream. I could not imagine telling—I thought that since it was a bad dream about him, I'd be at fault for having it.

I told him I was afraid I'd get in trouble if he knew about my dream. He said, "No, you won't. Of course not." His kind and gentle manner was a good thing at that moment. I will never forget the tremendous wave of heaviness, fear, and horror that welled up in me as I blurted out the dream. It was taking a real risk! After I almost exploded with fear—both in the dream and while retelling it—my dad reacted in a way that opened a new understanding for me about the power of dreams.

My dad's reaction was sudden and spontaneous: he found humor in it! What a surprise and a relief. I wasn't in trouble at all. At that moment, I realized something that has served me my entire life: dreams do not have to "own" us, no matter how big their impact is on the dreamer or how real they seem. Dreams cannot be denied, but they are not something that should destroy us or keep us stuck in fear. They are not something we can be blamed for having, either.

In my child-mind, I thought I could be blamed for my dream, but when I realized that dreams are *subject to our assessment of them*, it lost its power to horrify me. Suddenly, my nightmare became "only a dream." In a gentle way, my dad showed me how dreams work and gave me a way to cope with them. From then on, I could first feel their impact, then decide what I made of them afterward.

This was empowering—a little bit like being a film critic watching a movie made just for me. I continued to have cinematic, impressive dreams, but they never ruled me completely again. Instead, they showed me the fears and troubles I had not surmounted yet. Dreams served me content on a silver platter. I gained insights into many areas of my life I had not consciously understood. If I had not experienced this conversation with my dad, I may never have fully realized the potential in dreams to help me understand life, and my childhood may have been harder to bear.

Finding the Meaning in Dreams

My family loved Edgar Cayce, who was known as "The Sleeping Prophet." Our copy of a worn-out Cayce paperback became my companion in high school days. I read that Cayce went into a sleep-like trance and was able to heal people by answering the questions they had about their health and personal struggles. Each of his dream-state readings were recorded and are fascinating to read. (One thing I recall is that Cayce slept with a French book under his pillow and found that he could speak French the next day. When I tried to follow Cayce's example and slept on a chunky chemistry textbook, I only woke up with a sore neck, but it was a turning point for me. Cayce inspired me to start experimenting with dreams.)

Reading Cayce and having more discussions with my father (who was a practic-ing psychiatrist at that time) led me to understand that one of the most valuable ways to look at dreams is to locate the *feelings in the dream* and match those with *feelings you have in your waking life*. The dream's logic, scenery, or sequence may not con-nect, but the *feelings* therein may, and this is a most beneficial way to gain intuitive insight from dreams. You can find the quiet but compelling emotional energy that fuels a dream by locating that emotion, recognizing it, and allowing yourself to feel it. Ask yourself, "When have I felt this way in my waking life?"

For example, I dreamed I was in a place I have never been before. There were lots of unfamiliar people and a feeling of activity. It was daylight, and I sensed this was a kind of vacation spot near the sea—which symbolized recreation and relax-ation for me.

When I woke up, I might have said to myself that because the dream was not very notable; it was a "nothing dream," with nothing much to offer me. But when I sank into what I *felt like* during the dream, some real stuff surfaced for me. My feelings in the dream were of discomfort, the kind I try not to show in social gatherings. I had felt tinges of nervousness and mild anxiety. As I allowed myself to feel that nervous energy from the dream, I recognized it and located it in my waking life. I had the same anxious feelings during transitions, like when I started a new grade in school or didn't know anyone at a new job. The feelings were strong. I could then determine why I might have had the dream at this time, which was a seasonal transition from summer to autumn. I realized I had some anxiety and low-level nervousness run-ning along with me into the new season. The dream told me that I needed more rest in these transitional times. I was able to intuit the meanings the dream held for me and allow it to help me understand better what I needed.

Predisposing ourselves to engage with our unconscious by paying attention to dreams is healthy. Having an awareness of dream meanings, connecting the memo-ries and associations, and accessing our capacity for healing can help us remain free of illness or despair. Allowing the unconscious to surface and educate us keeps us free of emotional weight that is no fun to drag around. Being intuitive enables us to better see the subtle meanings and feelings that we might otherwise miss.

In processing dreams, we find that our unconscious and conscious thinking work together and our intuition (feeling and sensing) increases. Day and night—asleep and awake—seem connected and vibrant. Walking around in daylight feels like dreaming, in a way, as a heightened awareness takes hold. Something from a dream shows up during the day; we recognize it right away, because we're in tune with our dreamscapes. While we are sleeping, we have lucid dreams more often; our conscious mind acts like it's awake, saying, "Oh, I'm dreaming! This is interesting." Normally, we are so on-task in our lives that we overlook how dreams may clue us in to our environment's subtle signs and synchronistic events. Taking time to stream draw helps us stay in that realm where the unconscious can work with the conscious mind to keep us in a flow no matter if we are awake or asleep. We can experience intuitive signs and messages during the day as being very similar to the events or signals and information we get during our dreams.

One of the most rewarding practices I've found is to keep a dream journal and stream draw right after I wake up. If you remember your dream, you can also jot quick notes about it so you won't forget it. If you don't remember your dreams, stream drawing will help get you back into that unconscious-to-conscious flow. (See "Stream Draw Your Intention to Remember Your Dreams" later in this chapter).

It's Your Dream: Changing Dreams Midstream

We keep experiencing the same things in life until we learn the lessons they offer. Dreams seem to work the same way. Until we grasp what the dream is trying to tell us, we will keep having it. Once we have the "ah-ha!" moment, we are free of whatever was holding us hostage.

For example, after I got tired of a bad recurring dream, I decided to deal with it head-on. What I discovered was life changing. In the dream, I was being chased by a scary person through the neighborhood I lived in from the age of nine to thirteen. This horrible dream always caused me to wake up full of fear. The fearfulness followed me all day, too. So, I decided that the next time I had the dream, I'd change it. I wrote in my journal every night: "I *will* take charge of my dreams. I will *stop* the scary thing from happening."

One night I had the dream again: an attacker was chasing me through my old neighborhood. He was only a foot or so behind me. In trembling fear, I ran past houses, up grassy hills, and finally said to myself, "Hey, wait. This is *my* dream, and I don't like being chased!" And I turned to face the attacker. I kicked him as hard as I could. He doubled over. I ran into a nearby house and locked the door just as the man tried to open it. The dream ended with a great feeling of triumph and empowerment.

I woke up feeling stronger. That feeling followed me all the next day and beyond. In fact, this experience marked a real turning point in my life for a few reasons. The fact that the dream took place in a neighborhood I lived in as a child was a big message for me. I was very unhappy at that time: my self-esteem was demolished, I suffered culture shock and major changes in my family, and a teacher at school mistreated me. I could find no comfort anywhere. I realized that the setting of the being-chased dream was about my fears, my personal nightmare of having had my self-identity crushed. In the dream, I was trying to escape a threat; this is how I felt while I lived in that neighborhood. The dream told me that I had not overcome my feelings of being threatened. My fear and hurt still needed to be healed.

The dream presented me with a chance to face my past trauma and deal with it. Taking charge in the dream was my first step toward claiming my perception of myself and conquering what was holding me back. I got enough insight to realize that carrying around this fear and injury had caused me to become entangled in a relationship that only added to my fear. The dream gave me a beautiful chance to turn my life around. I ended the relationship that was not good for me. I consciously worked with my unconscious to feel more self-actualized and to create the life I wanted, and it worked.

If dreaming helped me to change my reality, contacting the same unconscious realm through stream drawing has had the same benefits. Only, instead of waiting for life-changing dreams to arrive, I chose to stream draw during the day while I was conscious. I began to see stream drawing as an act of intention, a true quest.

Safe Harbor:
How Does Stream Drawing Re-create the Dream Experience?

In my nightmare, I took charge by saying, "This is *my* dream and I don't like being chased!" When I stream draw, I say, "This is *my* stream drawing and I am in charge!" This sends a signal to the unconscious that says, "I'm aware of you and ready!" This allows me to open the channels of emotion and thought (often ones I didn't realize I had inside) between my mind's unconscious and conscious parts. With dreams, we mostly wait to see what comes, but in stream drawing we can actively get the flow going. The dream showed me I was harboring feelings I did not realize I still had. Stream drawing can do the same because we open a dialogue between the conscious and unconscious.

Dreams and Visual Imagery:
Empowering to the Intuitive Seeker

I am not exactly sure why intuitive stream drawing readings work, or how they manage to offer information to clients seeking guidance. The practice of doing intuitive stream drawings is similar to the way dreams work. They offer us a lot, if we pay attention to them. Dreams give us clues into our subconscious and often tip us off about what is coming our way. Dreams teach and warn us. They cause us to feel emotion. They are often useful, giving creative ideas and new perceptions, and we can use them to offer help to others.

I wrote my first book on intuition, *Illuminara Intuitive Journal*, because I wanted to show others how to use a method of visual-intuitive knowing that is natural and immediately available. I found that looking at images unlocks the unconscious memory, similar to the way dreams work. I realized that we have a built-in way to develop our own sense of intuitive intelligence through making marks, dreaming, and noticing the messages that arrive for us.

I feel passionate about showing people how to find their own intuitive process and spiritual connection. We have powerful reactions to visual imagery. If we listen to the intuitive voice inside us as we see images, we can develop an "inner library" of memories and intuitive sensing. Paying attention to that quiet inner voice holds so much healing, powerful, and transformative information. It's like dreaming: a portal to an expansive, ever-growing inner realm. We can tap into the same kind of imagery we see in dreams during our waking hours.

Beyond our personal benefit, we can do this *for each other*. While practicing intuitive stream drawing readings, I felt the same kind of enchantment and spiritual awakening as when I realized what a dream was trying to tell me. I recognized that collectively we are able to heal one another.

Through dreaming, journaling, stream drawing, and practicing intuitive stream drawing readings, we send a signal to our intuition that says, "I am ready for a revelation. I am expectant and joyous in the thought that dreams and streams of consciousness will help me in life, guide me, and make me aware." This brings a freedom of spirit. We begin to see connections we had not recognized before. They help us reach new heights of self-awareness and give us the ability to stream and dream for others, in ways that might help them.

We're In It Together: Dreams Connect Us All

I learned early on that dreams could guide me, and as I developed as an intuitive reader, I saw how intuition and dreams allow us help each other, as well. We're connected far more than we know. All we have to do is have a genuine desire to help someone.

Recently, I discovered the work of Dr. Henry Reed. He is known as "The Father of the Dream Movement." As the Director of the Edgar Cayce Institute for Intuitive Studies, Reed has devoted his life to dream study and experimental intuitive exploration. He developed an intuitive method called the Dream Helper Ceremony, where everyone participating dreams for a person who sleeps in "The Dream Tent."*

---

*Dr. Henry Reed, Edgar Cayce Institute for Intuitive Studies. www.eciis.org.

I took part in one such experiment, and the results fascinated and surprised me. Out of a group of eight people (all strangers prior to the event), one volunteered to be the dream subject. The rest of us were "dreamers." The person we dreamed for was a wonderful intuitive healer with a problem she needed help solving, though none of the dreamers knew her problem. With Reed's guidance, the dreamers formed a circle around the subject and vowed to dream in honor of her that night, so our dreams might offer her support. Without knowing anything about this woman's life, we all went off to sleep. When we woke up (in the middle of the night or first thing in the morning), we wrote down our dreams.

The next morning, we all sat in a circle and shared our dreams out loud. We still did not know the subject's problem. She listened intently as we each described what we had dreamed. There were unexpected and uncanny similarities in our dreams. For example, I dreamed I was on a bus, looking out the windshield at all my furniture outside. I knew I'd have to get off the bus and move it all inside quickly. How would I do this? In my dream, my husband was no longer my husband, and my son in the dream was not my actual son. Other people in the group dreamed of furniture being moved around and about family struggles.

After all the dreams were shared, the dream subject revealed that her problem was making a decision whether or not to stay in her marriage, whether she should move out of her life with her husband. Even without knowing her problem, we all dreamed something that could be helpful to her as she sorted out her situation. She could see that having to move her belongings from one place to another would be an ordeal, and that considering how such a change might affect the grown children would also play in to her decision. This dream experiment created healing for the dream subject and the dreamers. Trusting our unconscious minds to deliver what was needed, and sharing what came, made a big difference.

In my own experience sharing dreams or stream drawings, enlightenment arrives when we trust that the answers will follow our intention to seek them. We have an innate ability to tap into a wellspring of love, information, and healing energy. When we gather together with the intention to support each other, this ability is activated. We have only to choose to risk opening our hearts.

Do Your Own Dream Experiment

You can try dream experiments yourself. Connect with a friend and pledge to have a dream for her. Ask the friend to write her concern on a piece of paper and put it away. You don't want to know what the concern is; you are going to trust that your dreams will guide you. Meet the next day and tell your friend what your dream was about. Just trust it! Afterward, you can listen to your friend's concerns and discuss them. Try this a few times, perhaps asking multiple friends to dream in honor of one person. Perhaps you will create your own dream group. I recommend keeping a journal to record the dreams you have and how the experiment unfolds, especially when you discuss your subject's concerns. If you don't remember your dreams, read a bit farther in this chapter for some ideas on how to spark your dream life into action.

Try It! Create a Streaming and Dreaming Drawing

To capture the essence of a dream and hold it long enough to process it before it slips away, you will need a journal to keep at your bedside table. I suggest a blank artist's sketchbook, since you may want to make visual notes and sketches as well.

If you remember your dreams, you can create a streaming and dreaming drawing by recalling a dream and using the stream drawing process: closing your eyes, breathing deeply, relaxing, and drawing with your nondominant hand. *Draw with emotion!* Gaze at the marks you made and *trust any words* that come to mind as you draw or gaze. *Discover and connect*, write down any words that come to you, and concentrate on how those words may relate to your dream or the feeling in the dream. If the words don't seem logically connected to your dream, try to find a connection to the dream's emotional quality.

Acknowledging our dreams while also practicing stream drawing expands our intuitive awareness. When we dream, the unconscious flows to us (we can't help it). But getting into that unconscious or stream-of-consciousness state while we are awake is a little different. *We must choose to enter that state.* I believe that making the choice to stream draw sends a signal to the unconscious that says, "I seek to be more aware." It is simply a matter of opening our hearts and genuinely wanting to explore, create, and know. My depth of feeling and intuitive knowledge strengthen when I pay attention to dreams and devote some time to stream drawing each day. You might already do this (when you're on the phone, drawing loosely on the margins of papers or on scrap paper). If you do draw at any point in your day, pay attention! There is something profound and valuable in your drawings that could lead you to higher levels of consciousness, open you to better ways to solve problems, and allow your intuitive sensing to guide you.

An Example of a Streaming and Dreaming Drawing

Dreams reflect what we are going through, so paying attention to them can add emotional and spiritual depth to our experience. I had a big change several years ago, and during that time, a dream helped me understand more.

I dreamed that I had newly arrived in a place like Venice. I met a friend who was already living there. She was wearing a full-length gown. "Oh," I said with weariness, "do I have to get dressed up?" Immediately a boat arrived to take me to where my dress was waiting. A lean and impeccable man was waiting for me; I understood he had ordered the boat and arranged for my dress. He showed no emotion but was punctual and had a severity about him. He was very professional as he assisted and prepared me. I felt secure with him, and grateful that he could do so much for me. I was very impressed with his coolness; he literally had no emotion about him. He did his duty with precision, on my behalf.

When I woke up, I held the feeling of the dream in my heart and mind for a few moments. Then I got up slowly and picked up my sketchbook and a pencil. I quickly drew in my sketchbook the look of the man in the dream. I also wrote the details of the dream; as I did, I discovered how my life situation resembled what the dream was showing me.

First, we had relocated to a beach-area town and rented a small cape house steps from the beach. The water in the dream was like Venice, so that connected for me. The friend in the dream was also someone I knew in town. She was personable and fun to connect with, but when I had arrived in town, I was exhausted and under strain. I did not feel like "dressing up" or being social in any way. I just wanted to get through what I was dealing with. The man who helped me prepare myself in the dream was probably my masculine side, who proceeds without emotion. This inner masculine aspect was taking care of me. My experience helped me develop a proactive, nonemotional way of moving through a difficult phase of life. It was a time for me to do what had to be done, without drama. In my dream, I met the aspect of myself that could proceed in a dispassionate way (whereas I perceive myself to be generally more emotional).

I wanted to delve more into how I felt in the dream, which held a lot of the dream's message or content. I decided to create a streaming and dreaming drawing about it. I looked at the blank sheet of paper before me and closed my eyes. While closing my eyes, I re-entered the emotions of the dream and the ones that I still felt upon waking. At first the feelings were not very strong, but as I relaxed and took deep breaths, centered myself, and imagined the dream, the feelings became much stronger.

I Drew With Emotion: With these feelings, I drew until I felt I was finished. The main sense I had was how tired I was, and how I had switched off some of my emotions in order to get through that phase in my life. I felt grateful for that—the man in my dream made me feel organized and reminded me that I wasn't alone. I really appreciated him. I felt all this while drawing.

I Gazed: I gazed at the drawing (Figures 20a and b; see insert for color version) and immediately recognized an image of a person falling off a horse. At the time of the dream, my family had just moved from a rural area where I rode horses daily and loved it. I was thrown off a cantering, bucking horse and during the physical therapy that followed, I realized that riding horses, every day had kept me from acknowledging a serious truth: my family needed to relocate, so my husband and I could be closer to New York City for our professions. I was so happy riding in the open fields every day that I was disconnected from this. Literally, the horse "unseated" me, so I was able to move (unseat) our family. I knew we'd made the right choice to move closer to the city when I saw the image of a rider falling from a horse, right smack in the center of my drawing—even though the dream had no horse in it!

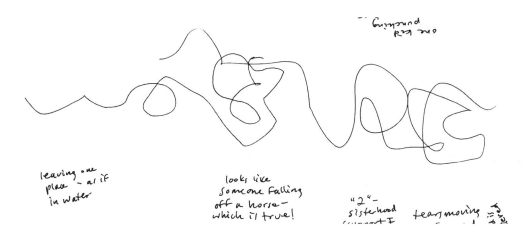

leaving one
place – as if
in water

looks like
Someone Falling
off a horse –
which is true!

"2" –
sisterhood
support I

tears moving

Figure 20a.
Original drawing I did.

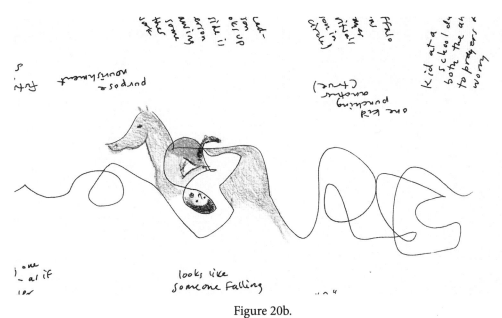

looks like
Someone Falling

Figure 20b.
My stream drawing of a person falling off a horse.

I Trusted My Words: I had no trouble trusting my words, but I still felt that there were some images in the stream drawing that I could not find words for. I decided to revisit the image later.

I Discovered and Connected: This streaming experience was easy to connect to my life. There were several other images that showed me exactly what was happening in my life at that time. The stream drawing validated my perceptions. I had built up endurance (symbolized by the horse) and been "unseated" into awareness (being thrown from the horse). Then, I had been able to organize and prepare for the move without excessive emotionalism (the precise, severe man in the dream). The dreaming and streaming drawing really validated that phase for me and brought it full circle.

Creating Dreams by Stream Drawing

Is there a dream you'd like to have? Up to this point in this book, you have read about how dreams can be better understood by stream drawing, and how we can even help one another by sharing our dreams. Now, you can use stream drawing to try and create the kinds of dreams you'd like to experience.

What is the point of trying to have a certain kind of dream? Is it only for fun? The point is that we have free will and can make choices in life—we create our lives far more than we realize. Getting creative with our dreams helps us deepen our awareness of the way our choices affect our lives. With practice, we will be able to create the life we most want to experience.

Try It! Conduct a Streaming and Dreaming Experiment

Now you will learn how to work with your dreams so that you can direct your mind to dream something specific. This exercise can be done alone or with another person. Stream drawing your intent to have a particular dream will involve the same steps as our earlier stream drawings. Make sure you have paper and pencil ready, take time to relax and stretch, and use your nondominant hand. Keep your eyes closed while drawing.

Write your intention at the top of the paper: "I Want to Dream About _____." Then draw with emotion, really seeing it in your mind's eye. If you want to meet your favorite celebrity in your dream (I've tried this before, and it really is fun!) or visit a place you've never been before, imagine this happening while you stream draw. Take as much time drawing as you need. When you feel ready to stop, open your eyes and gaze. What do you see in this stream drawing? Trust anything that comes to mind, and write it down. Discover and connect by going deeper. Make a note of any words that came to mind and see if you can make sense of them in connection with the images you see. Do some of the stream drawing images relate to wishes you've had or been denied? Take notice of any other images or feelings that arise while you're gazing.

Put the stream drawing down and look at it later. Do you see any other symbols or notice something you didn't see before? Before you go to sleep, create another stream drawing. See the dream you most would like to have in your mind's eye as you are stream drawing. Allow the pencil to help you feel the good feelings you'd like to have in your dream.

You may need to do this kind of stream drawing with intention for a few weeks, coupled with daydreaming during quiet intervals while you are awake (see and feel yourself doing what you wish to do in your dream). Daydreaming reinforces your intentions. Remember, this kind of intuitive knowing is a practice and a process, so be patient.

The dream may come when you least expect it. Or, if you're lucky, you'll have your dream-wish come true right away. Believe that this dream will occur, and you will experience it. The more you feel it as a true thing, the more likely it is to arrive for you. Once you have the dream, journal about it or stream draw to learn more about the meaning in the actual dream—or record it just for the sheer happiness of experiencing a wish come true!

If you'd like someone else to do a stream drawing for you, have them state the intention: "_____ would like to have a dream about _____." Find out what came up for your friend in her stream drawing. That person's streaming might offer you some unexpected insights. You can discuss your impressions during the *Discover and Connect* phase, talking over what may help or hinder you in the way of remembering dreams.

Stream Draw Your Intention to Remember Your Dreams

You might say, "But I don't remember my dreams!" Don't worry. This is a process, and there are ways for us to develop dream memory. If you do not remember your dreams, you can create a streaming and dreaming drawing in a few different ways to enable you to open up to your subconscious and begin to remember your dreams.

For this stream drawing experiment, I recommend using large newsprint paper. You will want to have lots of room to roam with your pencil, using the entire page if you like. Take a seat and be ready with your paper and pencil or pen. Close your eyes and begin to breathe deeply. Feel the emotions arise when you focus on your desire to remember your dreams. Do you feel aspiration and expectation? Do you feel frustrated that you do not normally recall your dreams? Do you feel nervous and unsure about how remembering your dreams might impact you? Do you just feel blank? Whatever your reaction, allow it to flow in and be patient with it.

State Your Dream Intention: Now, say something like this out loud: "I will remember my dreams. From now on, I will be able to wake up and remember my dreams well enough to write them down."

Draw with Emotion: After you state your intention, begin to draw with your eyes closed, using your nondominant hand. Hold on to your intention, and continue to say it aloud with genuine desire. Draw all over the page until you are finished. You will know you're done when you have a feeling of completeness. You get to decide when to stop.

Gaze: Once you have finished drawing, open your eyes. Now, as in the previous stream drawings and gazing sessions, allow your eyes to rest on the marks you made with a feeling of loving calm and joy within. Explore the visuals this drawing offers. Make note of anything familiar—shapes or lines that speak to you. You might see a head, an eye, or an animal. Take note! Allow yourself to have a generous, expansive view of the marks you made. Do any shapes remind you of anything? Do any lines feel particularly strong? Turn the drawing around so you view it from all four directions.

Trust Your Words: If words come to your mind, trust them. Get "dreamy" with them. Playfulness helps open the channels of imagination, so play with any words that come to you by writing them down and seeing how they may relate to each other. Let words flow out that describe what kinds of feelings you'd like to have in dreams, such as "sublime" or "adventurous." Write your wishes about the kinds of dreams you want to have and remember, such as "I want to have a flying dream," or "I want to dream that I'm going to Paris"; whatever you'd like.

Discover and Connect: Once words stream in, discover why they did. Connect them to your life and your aspirations. Since you'd like to start remembering your dreams, are any of the images in your stream drawing signs or symbols of obstacles? What might interfere with your ability to remember your dreams? You might get messages like "not getting enough sleep or exercise" or "not inviting dreams to come through." Do any of the images lend possible hints as to how to remember better? Are there any images that remind you of things that you deal with during the day, or with what you eat? (Diet and exercise may influence the dreamer.) Do you see anything in the stream drawing that reminds you of an animal? If so, what does that animal represent to you? You may also look it up to see what its symbolic meaning may be. Did you have any particular stream drawing emotions (how you felt while drawing)? Maybe you felt or remembered someone or something in your life—perhaps that person, thing, or situation is connected to a reason why your dreams are hard to remember. Pay attention to anything that comes to mind, and don't be embarrassed by any of it. All of it will guide you to capture your wish to remember your dreams.

Streaming and Dreaming to Music

One of the ways to break through barriers with streaming and dreaming is to use music while drawing. In the next intuitive exercise, musical influence can inspire us by activating our senses in helpful and powerful ways.

Music can shift our current thoughts and feelings and free us from restriction and limitation. Using music to evoke emotion is a powerful mode of opening to intuitive sensing. I have also found that dancing to music while stating an intention such as "I will remember my dreams," or "I will have a dream that I can change into whatever I want" is very helpful. Physically integrating your intention into your conscious mind by moving your body sets everything rolling in the right direction. If you think about it, prayers in many cultures involve some kind of physical movement. People kneel, bow, or make the sign of the cross, for example, before and after setting a prayer intention. They rock back and forth at the Wailing Wall. I believe ancient people knew the power in moving the body while praying—it gets the intention activated.

More Tips for Remembering Your Dreams

Drink Water: Some people say drinking water before going to bed wakes them up at night, and they remember what they're dreaming when they get up. You can try this if you like.

Don't Move: I have found that when I wake up, if I remain completely still (as opposed to hopping up and doing sit-ups or racing to get dressed), I sift through the dream I just emerged from. I can feel, see it, and partially re-enter the dream by falling asleep again. Try to stay still as you wake up. Then gradually and gently move as you reach for your dream journal and pencil. Write it all down, but stay as calm as you can, as though you are still in the dream realm. (I often write while still lying down, having grabbed the journal from my nightstand. It may not be as legible, but I remember better if I don't start moving around.)

Take a Nap: During the day, a dream from the night before often drifts back into my mind, taking me by surprise. The dream may be blown by me like a leaf, but if I lie down for a few minutes with my journal beside me, I can scrawl some words down without even looking. Usually it is legible enough for me to decode later. I can sometimes sink right back into the dream; once I have a note jotted down, I can recall it. It is in my memory, so I can access it again and remember even more about it.

Continue to Journal: You can revisit dreams you had decades ago if you write them down. You'd never remember some of them otherwise. But the instant you see notes and sketches of dreams you've had, it is remarkable how they come back. The insight this gives is amazing. A dream may show you more as your insight increases and matures. You can have some compassion for who you once were. Shadows of the past can cast a light on today!

Drawing Conclusions

We've explored how stream drawing taps into the unconscious in the same way dreams do. Like dreams, intuitive stream drawings can be understood in multidimensional ways. What we learn about ourselves through our dreams can be integrated with how we activate intention during waking hours through drawing. Streaming and dreaming keeps us in tune with our empathic knowing. We can better understand the messages and signs that point us toward a fulfilled life. We can stream draw to music, using the techniques we've practiced to recall or create dreams. Without even knowing another person's particular problems, we can stream draw in their honor; when we share what arrives, we can offer beneficial information to them. Integrating unconscious knowledge in our waking day keeps us in the flow. Enjoy streaming and dreaming!

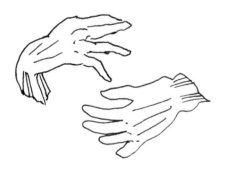

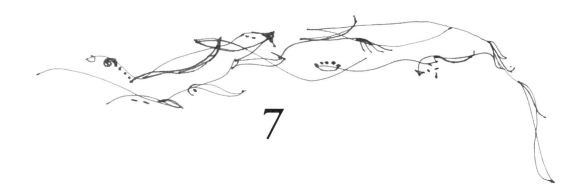

7

Visionary: How to Read a Stream Drawing

One day I went from doing an intuitive reading to *drawing an intuitive reading*. What followed—gazing into the drawing for intuitive knowledge—came as easily as breathing. The way it all came together was unexpected. In this chapter, you'll see how stream drawings can take on a specific structure and can be read and used as intuitive guides. The structure has evolved since I started out; I am sure it will continue to evolve over time. The ability to see and find meaning is multidimensional and abundant. As you explore creating your own stream drawings, and working with this intuitive method, you'll use all the steps you've practiced so far (*draw with emotion, gaze, trust your words*, and *discover and connect*). These steps will be combined within the basic format of intuitive stream drawing readings. You'll probably find that the step of discovering and connecting is very enriching, as I have found.

When I tried closing my eyes and drawing the first time I did an intuitive stream drawing reading, I followed an urge I had. I closed my eyes and drew; when I opened them, I began gazing at the drawing and realized that I could turn the stream drawing in different ways to read its meanings. As I practiced more, I saw that certain features always came up in the drawings. These characteristics are still fascinating to me. Though they offer me a kind of spiritual architecture, they are each unique as well. The structure I perceive in intuitive stream drawing readings gives me immediate guidance and information.

Characteristics of an Intuitive Stream Drawing Reading: How to See and Perceive

Think of a stream drawing as a two-dimensional thing that has no uniform structure. It is a wild image—an organic mishmash of randomly drawn lines twisting into shapes and forms. We cannot easily make sense of it, and need a way to organize it in our minds. We can impose a structure upon this random collection of shapes and lines, giving ourselves a visual reference. No matter what general shape the actual stream drawing may be (circular, oblong, rectangular, square), the point of reference we choose helps us perceive the randomness in a new way. With context, we can find the meanings in the image. In this method, we first use a *horizontal orientation*, a left-right progression. We gaze at a stream drawing and see it from left to right. This viewpoint allows us to perceive the drawing as showing us past, present, and future. The past is represented on the far left; the present is at the center of the drawing; and to the right we see the future.

After gazing with a horizontal viewpoint, we rotate the drawing a quarter turn counterclockwise, so what was on the left (in the "past" position) is now on the bottom. Now we can impose another visual structure upon the stream drawing, a *vertical orientation*. The image has a top, middle, and bottom. We can begin to see the drawing as a person, standing up, from head to toe.

Horizontal and vertical viewpoints help us assign meaning to the wildness of a stream drawing. It becomes more than a stream drawing, it becomes an intuitive stream drawing reading. Yet, even within this structure, there is still a random, organic quality to the process, not unlike dreaming. Intuitive stream drawing readings are multidimensional; they can be seen in so many different ways. Each time you gaze, another perspective will come into focus.

A Quick Look

The basic structure of an intuitive stream drawing reading gives us two views, which are explained more fully in this chapter:

- **Time line** (also referred to as a **life experience line**)—the left-to-right, horizontal view conveying past (left), present (center), and future (right)
- **Chakra chart**—a top-to-bottom, vertical view (seeing a body from head to toe in the lines and shapes)

There are also special features found in the time line and in the chakra charts in each intuitive stream drawing reading. The basic features are:

- **The Four Directions**
- **The Inner Child**
- **Duality**

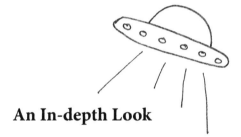

An In-depth Look

First, let's look closely at how a time line speaks to us, then at how a chakra chart works.

Time Line

The horizontal view of a stream drawing moves from left to right across the drawing and includes a visible time line that indicates specific, important life experiences. It may represent more recent events as well.

The time line view gives us scenes from life such as infancy, childhood, the present, and possible future. Usually, something in the far left side of the stream drawing indicates a childhood memory; the center of the drawing is "now." The future is to the right. (However, now and then, an entire time line will have only current life experiences and influences and nothing from childhood. I trust that whatever is most needed will come through. Just treat each reading as unique as each individual.)

The time line consists of a center point, which is where I start the reading, since the center can convey "what is important" or "what is going on now." I search the left side for significant past experiences and the right for future dynamics. This provides a full visual-intuitive spectrum of an aspect of the subject's life. I allow this to be a basic guide. Generally, the readings offer scenes and experiences from the past that we need to let go of in order to move forward. The images may convey or direct you to understand intuitively what is happening or what has happened. Usually people are ready for a bright future and feel distressed when things don't come together quite right. The time line can help tease out beliefs or attitudes that may have an impact on the subject. This gives the subject a chance to become conscious of anything that holds him back from the life he would most like to live. I believe the time line acts as a friend to help guide us through the lessons we've learned through time.

Chakra Chart

This structure or viewpoint is vertical and includes the special feature of a chakra chart. Turning to see the intuitive stream drawing reading from a different angle, you'll see it from top to bottom. The vertical view of an intuitive stream drawing is like looking at a person standing up. You can scroll down visually as you gaze. At first, you might not think anything resembles a person, but try to look at it this way.

The chakras are the seven centers of the body where we store emotional and spiritual life-force energy:

Crown Chakra: This is at the crown or top of the head, and above the head. Crown chakra relates to mental energy, consciousness, spiritual connection, and life purpose.

Third Eye Chakra: This is at the center of the forehead and signifies spiritual seeing and visual-intuitive consciousness.

Throat Chakra: This is located in the throat and is the center of communication for individual development and personal truths.

Heart Chakra: This chakra is located at the center of the chest. It deals with emotional growth, unconditional love, compassion, and inspiration.

Solar Chakra: This is in the solar plexus. It is the place where emotion and life experiences are processed. Here, life nourishes you through individual empowerment and perspective.

Sacral Chakra: This is located in the sacrum. This chakra is the place where creative life force and productivity (reproduction) resides with joy, pleasure, spiritual desire, and abundance.

Primal Root Chakra: This is located in the base of the spine (and lower in the body). Its functions are primal instincts such as desire, fear, survival, passion, anger, and sexuality.

Special Features

Now let's explore the special features that are a part of each intuitive stream drawing reading.

The Four Directions

After creating an intuitive stream drawing, I look at it by turning the drawing four times (Figure 21). Turning the drawing as a technique came about naturally. The

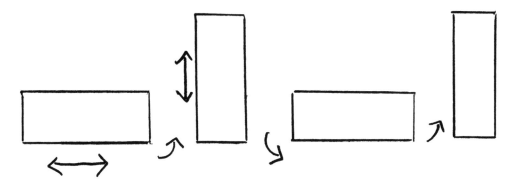

Figure 21
The four directions.

new viewpoint alters my perspective and helps me extract all of the drawing's potential information. It gives me multiple chances to absorb content. Keep an open mind and enjoy it!

As you locate the drawing's emotional energy, let your feelings guide you toward specific areas. I follow the same guidance for studying dreams while reading intuitive stream drawings. Your conversation with your subject about the feelings she has about the drawings will offer even more insight.

The Inner Child

This is a special feature of chakra charts. Inside a chakra chart, you may be surprised to see another smaller body, or several. This is known as the "inner child."

There is almost always at least one inner child present in the body of the drawing. The human figure you see as you gaze from top to bottom will have smaller looking human figures within it—which may look like animals or other things that represent the inner child. The inner child is the aspect of the self that represents a stage of life we once lived. It can be activated or triggered at any time. For example, in one reading, I saw an inner child standing on what looked like a box. She was holding a spatula. I thought the subject must have liked to cook or create as a child; I discovered during the reading that she grew up doing all the cooking for the family from the age of nine, when her mother starting going to work outside their home. Inner children help explain a lot about the subject's emotional disposition, strengths, and challenges.

The inner child lives with us, wherever we go and whatever we do. We have more than one, in fact—probably one for each stage of our childhood. Some are more prominent than others, depending on our experiences. Wounds and time periods when we found no closure are often what make an inner child powerful, as nobody experiences a childhood without some harsh episodes. We may not be fully conscious of the effects of those experiences. Maybe our needs weren't met as children. We may have suffered injustices that we spend the rest of our lives working on, getting over, or running from. Becoming conscious of our inner child is a pathway to release, forgiveness, and emotional rebirth. We learn to work with this inner child. If we do not, we have a two- or five- or nine-year-old (or an inner teenager!) making our decisions for us.

The inner child does not give up, so we have to develop a way to nurture and care for her, giving her a chance to heal as we nurture whatever aspect of the self cries out for attention. Like a real child, this emotional inner child only wants to be healed and happy. Once we become conscious of her urges and perspective, we are able to give her what she needs and stop allowing her to drive our agendas, relationships, and decisions without our conscious awareness.

The inner child also provides imagination, innocence, and an immense amount of creativity; this is often evident in the essence or feel of the inner child as it appears in the chakra chart. Much of what we do in life springs from our original sense of self, youthful ideals, and earliest hopes and dreams. This is evident in the intuitive stream drawings. We can embrace and love our inner child in order to fully understand what motivates us and how we operate in the world. We can reclaim that wonderful, creative spirit we once had, keeping it with us. The presence of the inner child in intuitive stream drawings is our fundamental guide.

Duality

Duality is a feature of intuitive stream drawing readings that gives us an inverted way to look at things, since there is more than one way of perceiving an image's meaning. Each image in the intuitive stream drawing will have a "shadow" and "light" aspect (sometimes I call them the "bonus" versus the "challenge"). I prefer to look at it this way to avoid using the word "negative," because I feel that word can be harder to overcome: when we are vulnerable, we are easily hurt by our own disparaging thoughts. Telling someone they have a "negative" in their intuitive stream drawing might harm rather than help the subject. Fear and anxiety undermine the potential to heal; instead of focusing on a client's "negatives," try to see challenges and wounds as pathways to clarity.

Duality is part of life. In stream drawings—and probably in everything in our universe—it's the yin-yang balance of it all. There is duality in nature, the things we've experienced, and our perceptions. My inclination is to take the shadow side of things (what is difficult and or perceived as "negative"), and use it as a tool for reaching enlightenment. We may have duality in this earth life, but we can triumph.

I do believe the purpose of hardship is to generate soul growth. The intuitive stream drawings are created with the intention to help see how all of life's experiences ultimately lead to enlightenment, strength, and deeper understanding of yourself as you experience fulfillment.

A Note About Recurring Imagery

You might find recurring imagery in different views of a single intuitive stream drawing reading. For example, in a recent intuitive stream drawing reading, my client had visual-intuitive images of pen and paper, letters, and writing over and over. In another one, there were repeated images of the number five, which for me signifies change—the end of one cycle, time to begin another (conflict and mobility). Paying attention to any image that repeats in a single intuitive stream drawing is important!

Shading and Coloring Intuitive Stream Drawing Readings

To help show the many ways I have seen into intuitive stream drawing readings, I have shaded (and colored) in some of the imagery. This should provide you with a visual idea of the intuitive information I got from the readings used as examples in this book. You can try this by photocopying your drawings and coloring in all the things you see in them, especially if it helps you remember the messages you interpreted. You may also have a partner look at one, ask him to shade in what he sees, and compare it to what you saw.

Drawing Conclusions

In this chapter, you have been introduced to the big picture: how to take a wildly expressive stream drawing and give it a structure, pick a viewpoint, and perceive its messages. It is now an intuitive stream drawing reading. You've learned a method of seeing that will help you make sense of the drawing's "random" quality. The stream drawings give a sense of learning through our lives in the time line, as well as helping us see how the body speaks to us from our emotional centers in the chakra chart perspective. You've also been introduced to particular features that are present and valuable when using the chakra chart method: the four directions, which gives you multiple viewpoints from which to intuit; the inner child that is present within each chakra chart; and the light and shadow aspect, showing the dual nature, with its challenges and bonuses.

Now, moving forward, you'll go on a journey to see how the process unfolds. Keep putting all the intuitive steps and structure together; next, you'll do intuitive stream drawing readings!

8

Seeing Is Believing: Intuitive Stream Drawing Readings

Now that you've practiced the basics of stream drawing and learned a method to give them a structure with particular features, you are ready to see how those techniques come together in intuitive stream drawing readings. This method of taking a stream drawing and gazing into it for intuitive guidance is based upon the visual-intuitive, empathic language you've been developing; now, you'll create drawings to function specifically as intuitive readings. All stream drawings are potential intuitive stream drawing readings because you can absorb their imagery in an intuitive way. However, intuitive stream drawing readings are stream drawings created with the specific intention of supporting another person, or solving an issue of some kind (for yourself or others). You will feel a deep sense of splendor when setting about to draw for the sole intention and purpose of making someone's life better or for solving one of your own issues. It is felt from the moment you state your intention—before your pencil even touches the paper. You'll feel flowing creativity while making marks on behalf of another, as well as discover that insights will be visible afterward and that stream drawing has a transformative effect.

Now, we'll explore some intuitive stream drawing readings that I created on behalf of clients. I will describe these cases the same way that you've been practicing your stream drawings, by breaking them down into parts. I'll show you what happened when I drew with emotion, the results of my gazing, the words that described what I saw, and how I connected parts of the image with each other, as well as my general feelings and impressions. Since much of this happens simultaneously, it probably won't seem as step-by-step as the process you've been learning. As you progress in your intuitive stream drawing readings, all the elements will begin to integrate: the gaze immediately brings connections and discoveries. While you trust your words, the information that comes to you brings you back to recognize something more in the gaze, and so on. You may even see some images in your mind's eye or get visual impressions while drawing. If the thoughts come to you, go with them! Trust them! As we move forward, keep the method in mind; what I will describe is still made up of the steps you have learned, just blended together.

Case Study: Endurance and Betrayal

This is an intuitive stream drawing reading I created for a client I had never met. It was a moving experience for me and the client because of the multitude of messages in it. I felt a special synchronicity with this client, as well. I had been watching a movie set in Hawaii and was deeply connecting with my memories and feelings of being in Hawaii when my studio phone rang. It was this client, calling to request a reading—from Hawaii.

Draw with Emotion: I closed my eyes and drew, feeling an inward sense of compassion for the client. I did not know the concerns or life situation of this person (most of my clients are complete strangers at the time of the first reading). I dedicated the stream drawing time to drawing whatever would best serve this client and said a prayer for guidance (part of my own process). I asked also to not only draw in honor of the client but to also interpret well the marks I made. I will show you four different views of the drawing and explain what I saw in it.

1. First Time Line: Past, Present, Future

First I look at the drawing in the position it was in while I drew it (Figure 22). I see what is in the center, which is usually very important, pertinent to "what is going on now" or symbolizing what is central to the person's life at the time of the reading. Then I look to the left for signs and symbols that represent significant childhood experiences. To the right, I see what is possible in terms of creating the future. I do not predict anyone's future for them, but sometimes get a window into it. My feeling is that we can alter, change, and create our future, and help ourselves be ready for the things that are to come. I like clients to know that they are in charge of their own future, rather than following what anyone else might say (friends, relatives, teachers, psychics) about how it will play out.

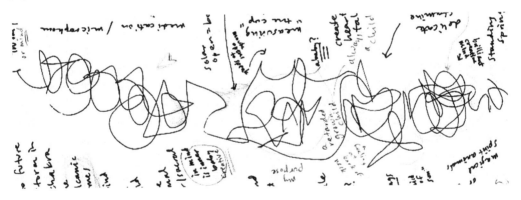

Figure 22.
First time line.

Gaze: Opening my mind to the wonder of the image, I gazed at the drawing to see what emerged. I kept my eyes wide but relaxed, drinking in the peripheral images as well as whatever I focused on directly. I continued to breathe deeply, and a feeling of expansion, enchantment, and excited calmness came over me. Specific things began to appear for me in the drawing, as though the drawing was talking to me or showing me what I needed to see. I colored and shaded in those sections so you can see how I saw it (see Figure 23; see insert for color version).

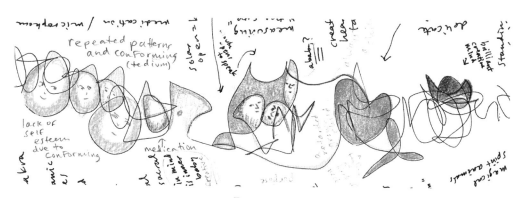

Figure 23.
First time line, colored in.

Trust Your Words: I saw a group of people in the center "now" position, shown here with three faces that have a red cape or wrap behind them, signifying "like-kind" or being involved in something larger or as a group. When I saw this, I felt that the client was dealing with some group dynamic issues. I saw gashes or sharp cut marks (in blue) near the group of people, indicating sharp emotion or actions—possibly a sign of aggression or of being "cut out."

I saw a heart near a flower, but there was a "heartstring" attaching the group to the heart (red line); the emotions of the heart were attached in a major way to the group dynamic, especially one member of the group. I saw a flower to the right of the heart and a little lower down, in the future position. To me, this meant that her heart would know new life, new hopes, and dreams come true. It also reminded me of a plane propeller, which signified travel and adventure.

I saw a buffalo head and horns (meaning abundance in Native American animal medicine) but it also looked like a cowboy hat, so I wondered if she'd live in the West or near real cowboys. I saw energy movement in the lines and a green leaf. The leaf symbolized newness, as well as health and happiness. In the "past" position to the far left, I saw people in line, like children, conforming in the way of dress and manner, suggesting a test of endurance and a denial of individuality. I saw a pill, indicating medicine.

I saw what seemed like a door—the client must have come through a change in the recent past, a significant change that led to her current situation. In the recent past, left of center, I saw a cup spilling over, turned upside down. For me, this meant that something of the client's was "wasted" in the group dynamic, since the cup is attached to the group image and is empty.

Discover and Connect: At the beginning of each session I tell clients that I will describe what I see in the intuitive stream drawing reading, and that this will include four different viewpoints. After I describe what I see, the client and I can deepen the interpretation together through conversation. So, before this client spoke to me about her life, I told her all the things I saw in her intuitive stream drawing reading. The client told me it resonated with her situation very much. She said she was dealing with having left an organization she created herself. Although she got it off the ground and was a founder, she'd been exiled from the organization in a way that she felt was very hurtful and dishonest. One of the members of this group was her husband (thus the heartstring from the group to the large heart on the right). She felt shocked at his betrayal of her. The client told me she was moving forward and still had strong emotions about the situation (also big heart), but was planning to travel (plane propeller) and possibly move (to California or some other West Coast location, validating the cowboy hat and the strong feeling of West Coast I'd had while gazing). She said she was looking forward to her future but had not finished grieving the drastic loss of something she had initiated and created, as well as the betrayal she felt; she felt the loss of trust and love from her husband and others in the group (cup spilling over).

The client told me that her childhood and school life was all about conforming, and that the school had a rigid culture. She never felt like she fit in. I believe I was led in the intuitive stream drawing to discuss the topic of conformity in her past because she was now dealing with having been cut out of a group. She was re-experiencing her childhood sense of not feeling included or recognized by the group at school. (Often, we live out life experiences in our adult life that are similar to those of our childhood. I personally feel that these patterns are "life lessons" and constructs that have something to teach me. The pattern usually stops repeating once the lessons are learned.) The client told me she was taking medication to help with the anxiety of being exiled from the group in her work situation (the presence of the pill in the intuitive stream drawing).

2. First Chakra Chart View of the Intuitive Stream Drawing

I turned the stream drawing to see it from a different angle (Figure 24). This time, I focused on it from top to bottom.

Using the drawing as a chakra chart, I see the formation as a human body, from head to toe. I see crown, third eye, throat, heart, solar, sacral, and primal root chakras: head, neck, shoulders, arms, abdomen, pelvic region, and legs. I can get a general feel for any physical issue or event that needs to be talked about. There is also always at least one inner child in each chakra chart. I have also shaded this one, so you can see what I saw in it.

Gaze: This is how I saw it (Figure 25; see insert for color version).

Trust Your Words: I saw a prominent inner child, facing the past with a sideways heart and flower at the heart chakra. There is also an arm and hand holding a blue pen or sharp object. This might be a sign of defense as well as creativity: defending what she creates. A large space (yellow)

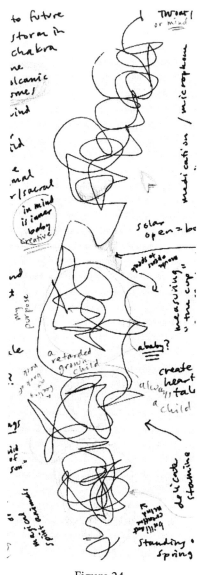

Figure 24.
First chakra chart.

filled the solar chakra, which symbolizes holding emotional energy and the desire to be "safe
at home." The primal root chakra is complicated
(lots of lines and shapes), but at the feet I felt as
though this inner child was full of energy and
moved around as though bouncing on springs
(green loop below foot). In the crown chakra, I
saw an opening shaped like a puzzle piece, where
air and light could come in. I felt this indicated
openness to spirituality and ideas. The circular
shapes turning to the sky (purple) seemed to
indicate devotion to connecting to divine energy;
there was also an eye in this formation, represent-
ing spiritual vision. The small pill for me (colored
green) possibly meant that medication was being
taken to quiet the mind or to deal with severe
challenges, represented by the shark's tooth (in
blue with the green pill), a sign for me that indicates treachery of some kind.

Discover and Connect: After hearing what I
saw in the first chakra chart, the client related to
what I described. She talked of having many years
ago created a healing organization that she envi-
sioned and was dedicated to. She put her energy,
hopes, and ideals into making her dream come
to life. She felt she was honest, good, and motivated to see her ideals come true. She felt like an
innocent "good girl." She created and advocated (the blue pen in defense position)
for her organization only to be betrayed and left feeling duped in her innocence. The
intuitive stream drawing reading reminded her of her ideals, her initial goals, her

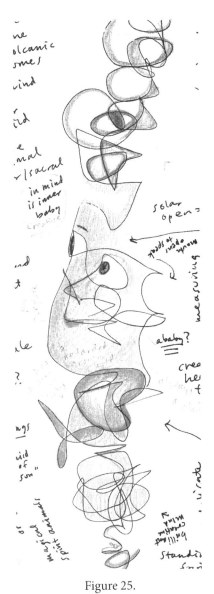

Figure 25.
First chakra chart, colored in.

mission in life, and how betrayal changed her life. Since this was the core concern she sought a reading for, we knew we were on the right path as we moved forward to discover and connect.

3. Second Time Line: Past, Present, Future

I turned the drawing again, so that I had another new vantage point (Figure 26). I had a second chance to read a left-to-right progression (past, present, future). I discovered this orientation functioned as a second time line.

Figure 26.
Second time line.

Gaze: This is how I saw the second time line (see Figure 27; see insert for color version), reading it as past, present, future:

What was in the "past" position in the first time line was now upside down, forming part of "future." Often our past experiences are repeated; they shape how we perceive ourselves, though we may not be conscious of it. When we unlock them, we can do away with what we no longer need and use what our past gives us in order to move forward.

Trust Your Words: I saw an elephant shape right in the middle (for me a sign of good luck) and two people close together, possibly mother and child, with a cup above them. One person was holding a pen or other writing or drawing instrument,

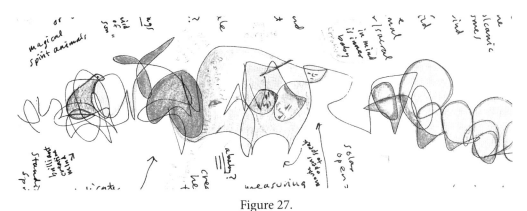

Figure 27.

Second time line, colored in.

signifying creative expression. The cup is in the upright position (rather than spilling over, as in the first time line view), which for me represented a relationship that would lead to prosperity in love and life. An upside-down heart to the left of center seemed to show love, but possibly confusion, too. A flower blooms again in this view, near the heart. It didn't remind me of an airplane propeller from this angle. To the left of that, colored in brown, is a sea lion or dog. For me, "dog" means loyalty. Sea lions are playful and curious. These two traits, I believed, might point to how the client enters relationships, with playfulness and trust. There is a phallic symbol to the right of the sea lion/dog. I took this to mean that in her romantic or sexual relationships, she is loyal. The phallus is drooping, signifying an impotency; this could be literal, or it could simply mean her mate is not present for her in a role that is sexually satisfying, or that she in some way is not feeling potent. It could also mean that the client's masculine energy is not aggressive.

To the right of center, in the "future" position, we have the little pill and the shark's tooth, followed by the rows of conforming characters or repeating patterns. The medicine in the future position suggested to me that perhaps the client might continue to benefit from medication as she progresses and creates her future. But this time, the repeated patterns reminded me of flowers, planted all in a row; I thought of how satisfying and natural it is to wish for symmetry or patterns. This is the desirable side of conformity, which makes habits and rituals that are delightful. I did note a small tear in between the last two yellow bulbs on the right, which for me seemed to point to the test of endurance required to tend a garden or sustain a necessary life pattern.

Discover and Connect: The client told me that she had a very special connection to her young child (which activated in many ways her own inner child). This parent-child relationship would require a future of repeated patterns (thus the garden and the bright part of keeping order in life), mixed with the angst—tears—which come as part of parenting a mentally disabled child. The client said she was writing a lot, and it seemed to me that attending to her child while expressing herself would not only sustain her in life, it would become her "Holy Grail" (the golden cup): an abundant, full future. The sea lion/dog symbol for loyalty and innocent playfulness was verified by the trust this client had in others, especially her husband; he let her down and cheated on her, abandoning the marriage (the drooping phallus).

The reading validated what the client was enduring and was an acknowledgment of how she had been cut out of a project she initiated, only to be left on her own to care for her child. However, she possessed what it took to express herself through writing and to work through the disappointment she felt. In the process of discovering and connecting, she felt stronger.

4. Second Chakra Chart View: head to toe, top to bottom

After seeing the drawing in three ways, I turned it again to get a fourth view (see Figure 28). This became the second chakra chart. It was an upside-down version of the first chakra chart view.

Gaze: This is how I saw the second chakra view (see Figure 29; see insert for color version):

This is the fourth and final way I looked at the intuitive stream drawing reading. As in the first chakra chart, there was at least one inner child, and some physical and emotional signals to explore.

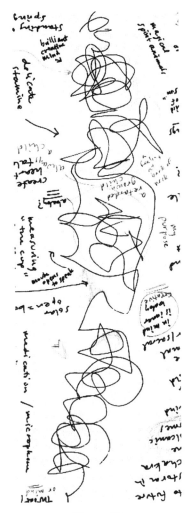

Figure 28.
Second chakra chart.

Trust Your Words: In this view of the second chakra chart, I saw a bluebird's head at the top, with the numbers 6 and 5. For me, 6 stands for feminine energy and group connectedness, the easy and the difficult. The number 5 represents mobility and change (of location, ideas, jobs, or other kinds of change). Bird formations are not unusual in stream drawings, and for me symbolize a range of things, usually individual expression, flight and freedom, or exotic character traits. This bluebird has two eternity symbols on its crown (the number 8) which in the crown chakra signify using mental energy combined with spiritual integrity to arrive at truths that transform. When I see an eternity symbol in a specific area of an intuitive stream drawing reading, I believe it indicates a clue to the person's soul path and purpose. Seeing eternity symbols in the crown chakra for this client made me feel that she was happiest when she used her mental or intellectual abilities. A colorful flower is at the throat chakra, along with a kind of spoon or cup, very like a silver christening cup a friend from Greece gave me when my second son was born (orange, to the left), which for me means being newly blessed. Because of its placement in the throat chakra area, it also meant that voicing her thoughts and opinions would be healthiest for the client; her expressiveness may have an impact that is a blessing in the lives of others.

Just below that, a very outraged person screams with a bulging eye and a wide-open mouth. This outraged being faced the past full-on. I felt that it indicated real anger and a deep need to vent. A small heart turned on its side in the jaw of the screamer indicated for me that the heart also wished to speak. This sign at

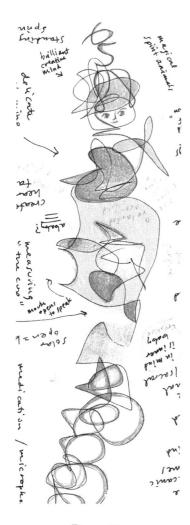

Figure 29.
Second chakra chart,
colored in.

this location in the drawing could indicate TMJ, or pain in the jaw from tension and clenching. Below this, to the right, a red shape reminded me of the back of the throat where tension might be held; it might mean the client was not feeling as though her thoughts and opinions were heard. A purple puzzle piece resided below the throat chakra, indicating that love was a mystery and there was more to learn about romance and intimacy. Another heart just below that, intertwined with the pill, seemed to me to say that her medication may be also used for the purpose of healing her heart, or that further heart healing is needed. Springs seemed to coil up from the bottom of the drawing like a jack-in-the-box, rather than showing primal root chakra details in the hips, tailbone, legs, or feet. This indicated for me that the client's experiences were shocking and had a serious impact on her.

Discover and Connect: I carefully communicated all I saw in this last viewpoint. The client talked about still having anger over the shock and humiliation of her recent crisis. The jack-in-the-box's wild impression made sense, since the client had great ability to initiate and lots of energy and vitality, but also since she was taking medication for the shock and pain she'd been through. Up above, the bluebird facing the past was singular and prominent. It felt to me like it wanted to be recognized as an individual. This client was ready to have a new phase of life where she could find "like-kind" and "birds of a feather" while also learning to live without needing the approval of a group to define her worth. The christening cup resonated with the client because she committed to getting through her crisis; she wanted to cleanse and renew her life's direction, in a spiritual way. She talked about needing to heal, release tension (TMJ), and take care of herself in her emotional and physical recovery.

Drawing Conclusions

In this chapter, you followed along during a specific intuitive stream drawing reading. You read about how the steps you've learned work in this intuitive process, as well as how the method's structure and features enhance intuitive insights. You had a chance to experience how a visual-intuitive vocabulary offers a way to perceive random shapes and lines in the form of viewpoints. We explored how two kinds of viewpoints, the time line and the chakra chart, give us an understanding of the potential meaning within stream drawings. Reading a drawing in the four directions, you got a sense of its duality; also, you saw how the inner child influences life experiences as we move through "past" into "present," while creating a future. Discovering and connecting the visual content showed how an intuitive stream drawing offers the client a chance to reflect on all she has experienced, gaining new understandings of important times in her life.

In the next chapter, you'll go a step further and create your own intuitive stream drawing readings, exploring this method more deeply. You will begin a practice of intuitive knowing that may profoundly affect your life, and eventually, the lives of others you read for.

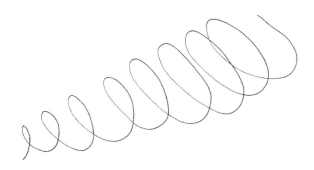

9

Streaming for Answers: Gaining Insight into Life's Questions

You've played with your perceptions while gazing at the personality in lines and shapes. You've done memory stream drawings that brought up emotions and explored the power of emotion more deeply in other stream drawings. You have tapped into your dream life and intuitive sensibilities through streaming and dreaming. And you've seen how intuitive stream drawing readings are structured and how to read them. Now, you're ready to embark on the next adventure on your intuitive journey. You'll really enjoy this method—it will help you find answers to questions and help solve problems!

This next exploration is about emotional energy and the power our feelings and thoughts hold over us. In this intuitive experiment, we'll let that power work toward our well-being by using it in a bountiful way. Let's say you have a real concern—one that weighs on you more than the others. You may not even be aware of it, but that takes a lot of emotional energy, whether you are constantly thinking of it, or working hard to avoid it (which could be more stressful than directly obsessing). Why not use all that emotional power to your advantage? It's there within; let it flow through! Using all that energy to make marks is a human impulse: it comes easily. Making gestures or marks as a response to feeling is part of our nature. In so doing, processing the meanings of those feelings becomes easier. Exploring the visual suggestions and meanings in our marks has real advantages, because we're communicating about those emotions. Choosing a natural form of expression (mark making) to get to the heart of the matter is really excellent because one thing is true: we cannot always control the problem, but we can control our response to it. In life, we will be subjected to situations and events that trouble us. Often, they involve other people, their choices, and institutions; we seem to have no way to alter or change them. However, we can use our free will to respond to challenges as we choose.

Stream drawing gives us the reflection time we need in order to know ourselves. After stream drawing, we can get centered and gain an objective point of view. We may have more self-control, patience, and understanding of the situation at hand. Making marks to gather up knowledge or to help choose the best way to respond or act is a very good practice.

In one intuitive stream drawing reading I did on behalf of a client, a great new way of seeing the past in relation to the present came through, giving the client a new perspective that really set her free of some misery. One area of her intuitive stream drawing, in the position of "past," felt emotionally shattered for me. I said, while gazing at this particular area, "Something's not right." I felt uneasy, nervous, and just not good when I looked at this portion of the drawing. I could not see an object or a specific image in that section—I only had an emotional response that was jagged and upset (see Figure 30; see insert for color version). The lines were broken and sharp. Their angles gave me a very unsettled, disturbing feeling. I knew that when I've drawn such lines, there is a broken feeling inside, such as anger or an out-of-control feeling. Those lines made me feel an "on edge," cracked, and nervous sensation. When the client came, she nodded in agreement while I described the shattered glass I saw in her early life. She talked about the severe abuse she encountered as a child—broken glass, knives, and other horrors. I knew then that the "something's not right" area of the drawing was tipping me off (just as dreams will do) to the incredible trauma this young woman had endured as an innocent child.

This client told me that she came in for a reading because she was terrified that she was in danger; she thought a ghost or some other kind of evil entity was after

Figure 30.
An image of sharp broken glass in an intuitive stream drawing reading.

her. She was physically shaking at the beginning of the reading. The more we talked about the intuitive stream drawing reading I created for her, revealing the trauma she endured at the hands of her mother's boyfriend (who used knives and was terribly violent), the more she realized that she never got over the constant fear she had felt as a child. She said she was once picked up early from school to wipe up blood from the floor after her mother was stabbed by this boyfriend. Her inner child was still traumatized and feeling unsafe, as though the threat was still there. The inner child was seeking peace, but feeling only fear. As we talked about the inner child's role in her current nervous state and what she had been through, she visibly calmed down. She said she had seen a psychiatrist, but he had not connected her past experiences as a child to her current feelings of terror. She left the reading with a new confidence. She felt calm and was relieved to realize she was not in danger at all, but had instead carried the full force of her childhood's true danger into adulthood—even though she was no longer near that violent person, or in an abusive relationship.

In another intuitive stream drawing reading, I reflected on a sense of urgency or nervousness I had, and it taught me how emotion can influence us, even when we don't have an answer for why it does. I did this intuitive stream drawing reading for myself based on a worry I couldn't let go of. It first arrived in a dream that made me feel like a world war was looming. I wanted to stop feeling that way. When I gazed at the stream drawing I made, I saw reflections of my concern in the drawing, such as warlike imagery of an animal caught in a net, but I also saw unlikely and seemingly unrelated things, such as a sombrero. I had not been thinking of Mexico, as being involved in a war, and almost shrugged the image off. But when I considered it further, I realized that the drug cartel wars were close to my home country's border. Those troubles resonate for me. Upon deeper reflection, I remembered a significant fact: I was born in Carson County, Texas, right in the middle of Comanche territory. I had recently read about how the Mexicans had fought the Comanche tribe for years before American pioneers arrived in the territory. Those pioneers were my ancestors.

I came away from the reading realizing that wars have always been part of our life on Earth; we *can* and do survive. Maybe I needed to face the fact that there will always be "wars, wars, and rumors of wars." I can still make life better in my own way, rather than stressing about global wars that I cannot control or stop.

Reading intuitively helps meanings to surface easily. This stream of consciousness conveys information about the situation I am concerned about, although it may seem unrelated at first. By staying open, I can let some light in, and those "random" images may serve me in new ways. Healing arrives through conscious, intuitive surrendering of logic. When your imagination and creativity work together, they become a source of coping strategies, and you can let go of your preconceived notions about whatever your concern may be.

I have found that blocks, obstacles, and unsolved problems in my life have to do with thinking the same things over and over. Sometimes I see things in black-and-white terms and refuse to let go of those ideas. If I hold so tightly to the one way I see things, I can't get relief or progress beyond the problem. In order to get to the solution, I need to activate my intuitive wellspring and get flowing with some new perceptions. It's simple: all I have to do is ask a question and trust what my perceptions give me when I gaze at the images I create with my eyes closed!

On another intuitive discovery, I may see two images in my drawing that have nothing to do with each other; each of those images may have a story of their own or a symbolic meaning that might lead me to deeper understanding. For example, animals tend to show up in my stream drawings. Horses are common. In Native American wisdom, horses symbolize power and endurance. The question I had when I created the stream drawing may require endurance or ask me to use my strength in a way I had not considered before. A horse may show me something personal as well, pointing to my own meanings of "horse." I keep all these associations in mind. I may also look up what other people in various cultures throughout time have said about the symbolic meaning of "horse."

Try It! Stream Drawing and Problem Solving

We'll do this exercise just like in the memory stream drawings and streaming and dreaming drawings. You will draw this time by setting yourself up comfortably with a blank sketchbook or paper (large or regular sized loose-leaf). Put all of yourself into this drawing method. Draw with the intention to pinpoint and solve a particular problem, one that holds your emotional energy and genuine interest.

At the top of the page, write your initials and the date. You may also write the question you have in mind. For example, "I want to know if it is a good time to change careers," "Will I ever fall in love again?" or "Why can't I get along with so-and-so?" Just be sure that you choose a question you'd truly like to know the answer to. The more emotional potency your question has, the more meaningful, focused, and authentic your intuitive exploration will be.

There is also another way to approach this. If you feel you do not have anything weighing on you much, choose something playful to ask about. Is there anything you always wanted to do or a person you always wanted to meet? You can ask questions like "Who was I in a past life?" or "Will I ever meet a famous person I really admire?" See what comes up. Often, during my intuitive readings, people want to know if someone from their past still loves them—that might be another fun question to ask while stream drawing. A question I like to ask, which is for me a form of prayer is "God, send me a message that you think I need to see and hear at this time." Try anything that feels delightful for you. Intuitive knowing derives out of our life-force energy, playfulness, and optimism. This is what creativity is all about. So get serious with your true desires or get playful—but don't stream draw with a question that holds little consequence or interest for you!

Draw with Emotion: Once you've written the subject of your problem or *project*— I like to say project because it sounds more positive!—or your playful desire to know something, breathe in deeply as you get comfortable. Get your pencil ready in your less-dominant hand. As you relax, begin thinking of your question. Close your eyes and draw with emotion. Allow the feelings and the energy of your question to fill your heart and mind. Let them flow through your limbs, out your hand, through the pencil, and onto the paper. Breathe deeply while you draw. You may cover the entire page, going back and forth, or you may just draw in one area. Draw whatever and however feels right as you embrace the feelings behind your question.

Gaze: Stop drawing when you are ready and open your eyes. Keep your sense of majestic calm as you gaze at the marks you have made. Allow that gaze to lift your spirit into a bird's-eye view over your stream drawing. Look for cues and clues. What do you see? Do any of the lines or shapes have a visual translation that connects to your question? Pay special attention to your childhood experiences. You may see something that reminds you of your past; it can help you figure out why you have this concern (or in the case of a lighthearted reading, why you have a specific desire). Do you get a particular feeling when you look at the personality of some of the lines or shapes? Take it all in. Explore the entire drawing. Turn the image to see it from all four directions. Look for inner children when you turn it to see the chakra charts. What do they tell you? What do you see in each of your chakras, from head to toe? Make note of anything that stands out.

Trust Your Words: As you find ways to connect the characteristics of the marks you've made with personal unconscious associations, meanings, and memories that have significance for you, trust what comes. Perhaps something makes no sense, such as "This loop looks like a melon" or "This reminds me of a fox, even though it does not really look like one." Trust it, even if it makes no sense or seems logically off-track from your question. It may even be more bizarre. You might see an area of your drawing and say "Tennessee" or "flying buttress" without having any idea why those words popped into your consciousness! Remember, during stream drawing the intuitive mind truly plays with our perceptions. Do not be afraid to go with the flow and simply trust what comes. As you move forward in your reading, do you sense a connection to the question you had? When things don't seem to connect, use your imagination and intuitive sensing to explore ways that you can connect them.

Discover and Connect: The next step is harvesting your discoveries. Once you've written what you saw and felt while gazing at this drawing (and perhaps notes on how you felt while drawing—thoughts, feelings, or mental images that came to mind), sit back and ponder its meanings. Let some time go by; you do not have to fully understand your intuitive stream drawing right away. I often create one, think about it, put it away, and then return to it later to see if I can "see into" it or comprehend its message over time. Look for the connections that arise in your drawing and in your day-to-day life; notice any synchronistic occurrences between your drawing and events in life. Trust that your perceptions will inform and guide you.

If you've asked a question based on a problem you'd like to solve, be in the flow while you receive any visual-intuitive information about it. Accept whatever comes into your mind, such as dreams, sayings, conversations, or specific people. Meditate on where the connections are, why those things came up, and how they may relate to your question or concern.

Drawing Conclusions

In this chapter, you've had a chance to dive into your own stream of consciousness. You've learned how to get into your stream-of-consciousness thoughts while creating with the intention to solve problems or seek answers. You've seen how a playful, open approach to emotional drawing can serve you very well; you can also help free the spirit of another person by doing a stream drawing in their honor. By nurturing your curiosity, you've used stream drawing to perceive new ways and insights. In the next chapter, you'll use all you've learned as you continue your practice of stream drawing to create intuitive knowledge. This time, you will center your emotional focus on another person and use your creative willpower to support others.

10

Celebrating the Lives of Others through Stream Drawing

Stream drawing for others is a way to acknowledge and honor their experiences and gifts. Intuitive information that is helpful to others arrives effortlessly when it is brought forward with compassion and empathy. By simply sharing information, we receive insights and possible new approaches to problem solving, as if by magic. Answers are not "somewhere out there," and they are not secrets: they are waiting to be discovered within us.

Since you have learned each step in the intuitive stream drawing method, and have practiced the skill in various ways up to this point, why not try using this intuitive process to help someone else searching for an answer to their problem?

Finding the Right Partner

First, you'll need a willing candidate. Consider going to a supportive, trusted friend. This will help ease you into being natural while developing confidence in your intuitive skills.

Use your intuition as you search for your partner. Not all people in your life will be open to your intuitive quest; it may not be the path they choose. Even those you love the most may not be able to do this with you. That doesn't mean you are right and they are wrong, or vice versa. We can respect each other without inviting injury. We can keep an open heart while also honoring our intuitive intelligence and surrounding ourselves with people who support our growth and well-being.

I recommend trying this skill with friends who are open or committed to deepening their empathic, intuitive knowledge. Do your intuitive exploration with someone who will respect and enthusiastically support you on this adventure.

It's a Win-Win Situation: Being Aware of Vulnerabilities

When you start to stream draw for others, a certain quality of vulnerability or shyness may enter your process. Once you become willing to share your insights, you have the power to enlighten others in unexpected and creative ways. However, depending on your delivery and outlook, sharing your perceptions can come across as supportive or deflating. Let's explore this aspect of doing intuitive stream drawing readings.

Being intuitive means exposing emotions. We are in a state of openness. When we open our hearts to others, and trust our words, or show our true feelings, we risk being judged or being perceived as less-than. Exposing our truth may seem weak, but that humility or vulnerability is actually strength: in being open, we are showing courage.

Why are kindness and compassion considered signs of weakness? Maybe it's because in the primitive brain, dominance is the key to survival. With this primitive mind-set, each human encounter has a "winner" and a "loser." Every time two people encounter one another, that dynamic is at play; automatically responding this way ruins our empathic power to connect with others without judging or labeling. While this win-or-lose dichotomy may be an undeniable part of our human presence, there are other ways to thrive on earth—compassionate interaction is one way. I believe that attaining a mind-set that does not require winners and losers is blissful because it is not based on fear and loss.

Looking at one another as cocreators can enhance a feeling of well-being and connectedness, especially when making intuitive stream drawings. Humans need to feel safe and at ease in order to maximize cognitive processing, learn, and grow with a sense of peace. I spoke recently with my friend and mentor psychologist Dr. Laurie Nadel, author of the celebrated book *Sixth Sense: Unlocking Your Ultimate Mind Power*. Dr. Nadel researches the effects of competition on the brain. She says that "the reptilian brain, the center of patterns, habits, and routines, sends out distress signals to the rest of the whole-brain system whenever it feels fearful or unsafe. This disrupts our ability to think logically or creatively." She further explains, "according to Dr. Paul MacLean, former chief of brain evolution at the National Institute of Mental Health, when the reptilian brain gets triggered into 'fight or flight' mode, it impedes any type of mental activity."* This means that becoming conscious and choosing empathy over "winning" is part of the process of intuitive interplay.

So when you begin building your intuitive senses, you need what anyone needs while learning, what we all deserve: support and encouragement. Knowing who to share your creative and empathic journey with is a way of setting up a fundamental, substantial, and emotionally safe environment. Positioning yourself for optimal growth by getting exposure to positive influences is essential. Using intuitive intelligence to heal has everything to do with respect and empathy. Daily life will also deliver us many people, places, and circumstances to help us develop empathy, inner strength, and intuitive sensing and processing.

Your Intuitive Partner Is Vulnerable, Too

I cannot emphasize enough how vulnerable your intuitive partner may feel. The reason I conduct intuitive stream drawings for others is to help them develop their own intuitive guidance, find healing, be enlightened, and love their lives—as they create the lives they most wish to live. I want this for myself as well.

In practicing intuitive stream drawing readings, I believe in always taking time to consider the most positive approach. Being open to asking the subject questions

---

*Dr. Laurie Nadel (coauthor of *Sixth Sense: Unlocking Your Ultimate Mind Power*), in discussion with the author, 2013.

(even asking them what they see in the drawing) will help you both understand what you see and sense. Including the other person in your reading is more generous of spirit than making statements that might give her a harsh thought—the kinds of thoughts that are hard to exile from the mind. We have a responsibility to make the process feel safe. We are only interpreting. We can be true to what we perceive as long as we find the duality in it. We can express the good side—the bonus of what we might see—as well as the bad side or challenge. Doing the reading this way gives the subject a chance to adjust, especially if your interpretation brings up difficult child-hood memories. For example, someone who experienced abuse of some kind may feel abused all over again if they're pressed to have a discussion about it before they are ready, or in a way that makes them feel hurt. We have to open the door gently, as we'd like a reader to do for us.

In daily interactions with others, it is not hard to express something in a clumsy way or to say the wrong thing; that is just part of being human. Sometimes, while I'm sharing what comes up for me in an intuitive stream drawing, I worry that I might say something the wrong way, which might be hurtful, rather than healing. I try to learn more every day that I practice this method.

For the one doing the reading, this is a tool for empathic connection. This method and practice offers a way to enlighten the reader as much as the reading partner. Our interpretations of an intuitive stream drawing are as much about us as they are about the person we read for. After all, our interpretations are subjective: we project our ideas outward. In that spirit, interpreting these intuitive stream drawing readings is a mutual endeavor.

Framing Your Findings in a Positive Way

I try to be positive about what I see in each stream drawing. Even the hardest events in life can offer something good, though that can be very hard to believe. For exam-ple, in an intuitive stream drawing session I saw the image of a car crash next to the image of an interior of a church (Figure 31; see insert for color version). I told the client that she might be involved with a church, and that the car crash offered a lot

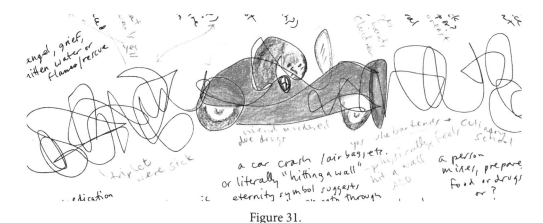

Figure 31.

An image of a car crash in an intuitive stream drawing reading.

of interesting symbols. This was a very disturbing image, but instead of saying, "This means you or someone you love will have a car crash," I said, "I see a car hitting an obstacle, and it can have several meanings. It could be literal, or it could mean that you need to use caution while you're moving forward in life."

Even though I may have premonitions and actual imagery from intuitive stream drawings may sometimes come true, I personally do not believe the future is etched in stone. We influence it each moment with our choices and intentions. There is a great mystery to why things evolve as they do. What good does it do to scare someone? We are not omnipotent interpreters. Some might argue that it would helpful to know these chilling predictions, but my philosophy is to describe what I see, not necessarily determine with absolute assurance what the image conveys. My promise to myself is never to do harm to someone seeking guidance and intuitive direction. It is essential in doing these intuitive stream drawing readings.

Later, I learned that the client who had the car crash in her drawing lost her father in a car accident a few weeks after the reading. She told me that the reading helped her cope. She felt that God was communicating with her about the terrible tragedy before it happened; after the fact, her faith was a comfort. The reading suggested she'd be inside a church—and she was at the time of the reading not at all interested in church. However, she recognized that her father's passing had involved her with funeral arrangements, prayers, a chapel, and lighting candles. I cannot say that the image in the intuitive stream drawing was a definite prediction. It may have been happenstance. I share the story to show that even major, sad, and awful things happen in life. Although they may appear in a stream drawing, I cannot say that they necessarily literally predict events. But I was very glad the intuitive stream drawing gave this client comfort and a feeling of security in her deepest grief.

If you see a break in a backbone, spinal curve, or other visual mark possibly indicating surgery in your drawing's chakra chart, you have an opportunity to talk about the subject's physical health. You might say, "When I look at this chart, I notice a mark on what I see as the spine. Does that mean anything to you? Do you experience pain there?"

Your intuitive partner will talk about whether this is accurate or resonates. If she answers, "Not really. I don't have back pain," move on. You might try to see other ways of understanding that particular image. If you and your partner wish to explore the symbolic meaning in back imagery, it might lead you to some important points. Could it be she carries a heavy burden in life? (You've heard people exclaim when they're tired, "I'm breaking my back!") Being open to the impressions your intuitive partner offers is fundamental. It is more empowering to discuss possible meanings together than to jump to conclusions that may be negative (and wrong). Saying "Well, I think you're going to break your back in the near future because I see a crack in the line I drew" is not helpful. Your words may do more damage than good because they put an image in the person's mind that is hard to get rid of. Another thing to remember is that people do not necessarily connect with intuitive-psychic input at first. Many times toward the middle or end of a reading, a client will remember, "Yes! I did injure my back in seventh grade." Everything will be discovered in its own time. Anything truly important will surface again and again, until we "get the message."

What about the other option in this case? The subject says, "Yes, I have had back problems." Then, you can use your intuitive meditation to help focus on how this back pain came to be, how to adjust life to remedy it, and discover ways it has shaped the subject's life. Is the subject's body talking to her by expressing emotions through physical symptoms? Is the subject working a job that stresses this area of her body? Did the pain come from an inherited trait? Find ways to help the subject change what hurts and heal what needs to be healed. The purpose of intuitive stream drawings is to start a person's momentum toward health, well-being, inspiration, and creating the life they want to live.

Intuitive stream drawings help us discover hidden or overlooked meanings in life. We learn from the marks we've made in life up to this point, literally, by living day to day. Our marks on paper help us remember what we forgot we knew. We are liberated from past traumas that prevent us from savoring a joyful present and glorious future.

Our personal truth—our vision for our past, present, and future—is ours to own. I urge you to be conscious of how you share your interpretations with others. Each subject trusts you to share what you perceive that may be helpful. Remember that intuitive stream drawings are not to be used as tools for domination or fear. Everything we stream draw is as much about us as the client, so we are equals in the process. We may have varying dimensions of being—we are each unique and on our own path—but neither person is a guru with a more brilliant connection to a source of conscious revelation than the other. Some of us may devote ourselves to developing that connection, but we all have the same potential and capacity for enlightenment.

Not So Helpful: "I see negative energy in your solar chakra."
More Helpful: "There is activity in your solar chakra; do you feel emotion or discomfort? This could indicate having pain in that region, or maybe surgery."

Not So Helpful: "I see a skull, so somebody is going to die."
More Helpful: "I see a skull image, or what looks like one to me. Let's explore that. It can mean many things, such as death or fear of death. It can be a sign of the end of one cycle and the beginning of another."

Not So Helpful: "I see you were abused as a child."

More Helpful: "The imagery here indicates something really hard to go through—it gives me the feeling of violence, aggression, or something unfair or difficult for a child. It could be literal or symbolic."

Not So Helpful: "I see dark patches here. It might be cancer."

More Helpful: "There are marks that indicate some kind of activity. This could be an illness you had or a new opportunity for healing something."

Not So Helpful: "Wow, your future looks bad, really bad."

More Helpful: "We all have good days and bad, and you will have a chance to get stronger as you move forward. Challenges open us up to learning new strengths and to use what we've already learned."

Preparing Yourself to Stream Draw for Your Partner

Just as in Henry Reed's dream experiments, the partner you interpret with does not have to tell you his issue or concern! I do intuitive stream drawings daily for people, never knowing their questions first. Most of them are people I do not know at all and have never met. They come from all around the world. Simply ask the subject to concentrate on their concern before and during your intuitive stream drawing. Personally, I like to open up my heart and mind in a certain way before doing a stream drawing for another person. My way is to say a prayer asking for guidance while I draw. I ask for the most helpful imagery to arrive on the paper, and for my interpretations to benefit the client as much as possible. Prior to each reading, I spend about half an hour in meditation on behalf of the client. I draw and then read the drawing to discover the images in it. Once the reading starts, I share what I see in the drawing, reading it in the four ways I have shown you (two time lines and two chakra charts).

You will develop your own way of approaching intuitive readiness to open to another person. Allow compassion to come to you via making marks. As you are sharing your visions, your partner can share his concerns. This is the *Discover and Connect* phase of the drawing method. This phase is a delight, enriched by your subject as he describes how he relates to your connections, making even more connections and meaningfulness. This builds a mutual fund of intuitive knowledge and may bring a lot of surprise and joy to the process.

The Emotional Weight of a Stream Drawing

Often, an intuitive reading starts with a question, usually, "I have this problem; can you help me with it?" Or the client may sit silently, waiting to see and hear what the reader comes up with.

I prefer to ask them *not* to tell what the concern is. That way, the *Discover and Connect* phase feels a little more exciting. The connections often relate to a person's concerns in surprising ways, giving them a new way to look at things. You may know your intuitive partner pretty well and already have an idea of their concerns and challenges, but try to work without specifics or information from your subject.

So when you and your intuitive partner begin a stream drawing reading with a question in mind, know that its quality and emotional content may weigh significantly on the outcome of the reading (whether or not you've been told what the issue is). Heavy emotional issues give an intuitive exercise real substance. Other times, it will be lighthearted (such as when a subject is holding her question with playful curiosity in her mind instead of dread). You will have to experiment with your own process to see which kind of theme has a better intuitive outcome for you. They may both work well for you—super-serious or fun and entertaining—but to start out, go with what makes you feel comfortable. You'll gravitate toward what feels best.

In other words, having fun and approaching the exercise with a spirit of whimsy might create a feeling of no pressure. You both go into the exercise knowing this. Or the opposite may be true: a deeply important theme or concern might help you emote and stream draw more effectively, as it activates your empathic expression. Finding out which type of mark making really works for you at this stage of intuitive stream drawing is interesting!

Let's suppose your partner has something on her mind that is only a fun question, the kind that holds curiosity and not much fear or worry. She may ask, "Will I ever go to Italy?" or, "Does the guy I'm attracted to also find me attractive?" Seemingly playful questions might actually carry a lot of emotional content, but you'll have to see how the process unfolds. Trust that your drawing will deliver what is most needed, if you dedicate yourself to being open and flexible in your interpretations. We are not infallible, of course. Our impressions are only one perception; there may be several other ways to interpret the same marks.

A subject may have a more emotionally significant concern. For example, someone might be upset about a marriage or social situation. Their question may be very important. For example, "Why does that person at work make my life miserable?" There is more emphasis on raw feeling in this kind of question, which means more emotional power. Use your intuitive connection to this person while you concentrate on opening from the heart and ready yourself to draw. Your intuitive stream drawing interpretation might be more potent and feel "right," even though you did not know the question. Your partner's seriousness and quality of urgency may motivate you to discover how to free her from that unhappy place.

The situation may be a serious life-or-death issue for your partner. In that case, be ready to understand that everything you say in your interpretation of the drawing has real meaning. Your words can be very important, building up the other person or diminishing him or her. Whether you mean to or not, your interpretation can injure someone or help heal them.

Also, please note that your partner's attitude and degree of openness may have an effect on how you share your interpretations. Your partner may feel rigid and dismissive. She may not wish to confirm or play with the meaning and purpose of your message. She just might not feel comfortable or open at that moment. That may make you feel a little discouraged or less in the flow. Sometimes, my clients remain stony and silent until the middle or end of the reading; then they become expressive and talkative. They relate all that the reading meant to them. I think, "If only they were so open during the process, we might have discovered more deeply what these images convey."

Trust that everything happens as it should, though. Understand that if your intuitive partner is not comfortable or you are not able to read for them, take it as a sign to try with someone else or to try again another time. Don't let any difficulty sabotage your efforts.

Try It! Stream Draw for a Partner

Choose an intuitive stream drawing partner. Ask him to hold a question in his mind without telling you what it is.

Draw with Emotion: Hold your pencil in your less dominant hand, paper ready. Breathe in deeply. As you relax and close your eyes, feel your heart chakra opening from the inside out. See yourself breathing in light. Pure and sparkling, it comes from above and moves through your body. See the light as it streams toward you, filling you with warmth. Envision it flowing from your heart to each of your limbs, to the ends of your toes and through your fingertips. Appreciate its beauty as it flows through your throat and third eye, all the way up to your crown. Keep breathing deeply and slowly. Open your empty hand and lift it up toward the sky.

Think of your subject. In your own words, ask for guidance and love to fill you as you draw. Compassion is the way to open up intuitive sensing for another. Experience empathy, the soft emotional nuance of caring for another person. Your partner—the subject of your intuitive stream drawing reading—is in need, and you are drawing in her honor. Feeling for this person and knowing that she may be struggling, ask to receive the images that will best help her. When you are ready, draw with your eyes closed. Allow the pencil to go wherever your hand moves it. Hold onto your thoughts and feelings for your subject as you draw. Keep breathing slowly and deeply. Once you feel that the drawing is done, stop and open your eyes.

Gaze: Look at the marks you made. Feel compassion for the marks and for your creative gestures. Open from the heart while gazing at the drawing. Continue to breathe deeply and slowly, feeling the wondrous light fill you as you allow yourself to simply take it all in, without judging it. Use your peripheral vision as well as focusing your eyes on the drawing to see with complete openness. Hold on to the feeling of empathy you summoned while drawing. Think of how the picture you created may be helpful for your partner. Write down whatever signs, symbols, or images you recognize or associate with meanings. Stay present while you gaze. You may realize that you feel an emotional charge, even if you don't see evidence of it in the drawing. Trust your feelings and make note of them. Often, intuitive information is not logical—but you know if you feel it, and it is important to honor that. Turn the drawing in four directions, seeking the message in its visual language. Enjoy what you discover. Trust the flow as you open yourself to gather empathic knowledge.

Trust Your Words: No matter what comes to you in the drawing, trust it. Whatever thoughts or feelings you have while gazing at the drawing, trust them. Do not second-guess yourself. Instead, simply continue to write down your interpretations of the imagery that surfaces in the marks you made. If you see an animal, for example, just write down the type of animal you see, such as "cartoon rabbit" or "chess horse." Later you can explore the symbolic meaning of the animal, but for now, write whatever comes to heart and mind as you gaze. You may write information down quickly just to get the sense of it, and you may reword how you express your impressions during the session, so you can use the best words. It's important to trust what comes to you, even if you think the idea is silly. (I am often surprised; one time, I saw a fiery plane crash in the "past" position. I thought it might be way off base to suggest my client had anything to do with a plane crash. The subject pointed to that place on the time line and said, "Yes, my mother and brother survived a plane crash. I refused to get on board prior to takeoff." It turned out to be exactly as it was drawn. If I had ignored this sign because I felt stupid for saying it, we would have missed an important intuitive validation.) Nothing is absurd or silly. All of what you perceive may have meaningful resonance.

Discover and Connect: Sitting with your intuitive partner, put the drawing where she can see it. Explain that you meditated on her behalf and drew while in meditation. Tell her that you will describe what you saw in the drawing and share what came to mind when you saw it. Also, explain that more images may surface during the course of the reading. Ask your partner to make note of any associations you derived from the intuitive stream drawing; if you like, ask her to gaze at it as well to see if she sees anything (some people are very interested in this—others, not).

At this point, do not worry about reading the drawing like a time line or chakra chart unless you feel moved to do so. Instead, simply turn the drawing in all directions, sharing what you learn with your subject. It may seem very general and unspecific, but trust what you see. Remember that the signs could have personal meanings or could help reveal truths for the subject. You may say something like, "I see an arc that really reminds me of a rainbow or a bridge. That makes me think of wishes coming true and important transitions or crossings in life. Do you relate to this, in terms of your concern or question?" As you discover and connect with the subject, she may wish to tell you what her issue is. You can go from there, making connections and sharing what feels meaningful.

Case Study: Love and Grief

Before you read any further, I want to share with you the very first case study of an intuitive stream drawing I did in honor of a client.

In my practice as an artist and as an intuitive reader, it is my mission to help heal the person while sharing the realization that within each of us is the power to heal and be enlightened; healing *is* an enlightened process. In my intuitive readings, I was using a combination of cards and visual intuiting (seeing images in my mind related to the client, like watching a movie during a reading). One day, prior to a scheduled intuitive reading with a complete stranger, I felt the urge to go into meditation and draw for the client as part of the reading. The urge was so strong that I knew I had to do it. I closed my eyes and said a prayer in honor of this woman, asking for guidance in creating the drawing for her. I did not know her and had never spoken to her before; I only knew that I wanted to offer her an hour of insight that would support her growth in life and potentially give her what she needed to create the life she wanted to live. I hoped my reading would get us talking and release her from any constraints, burdens, or anything holding her back from happiness. I wanted the reading to unveil her personal truth and give her what she needed to become more fully conscious. I asked in prayer for any helpful information to be delivered onto the paper, through my hand.

Feeling a sense of wonder mixed with an emotional, expansive feeling, I took a deep breath and drew with my less dominant hand. I drew using one continuous line that went all over the paper, twisting into shapes and forms. I went from left to right across the paper, following what felt good and "right." I cannot explain how I knew; I allowed the drawing to happen, and I knew when to stop.

What I saw when I opened my eyes and gazed at the page with the drawing in Figure 32 was powerful. The lines and shapes came to life for me as a visual feast. In my mind's eye, and with my heart's eye, too, I saw much more than just lines and shapes scrawled on paper. My eyes first rested on a shape that immediately reminded me of a grandmother. She was lying down. I do not know why it reminded me of a grandmother, but I accepted it without second-guessing. She looked like she had some kind of trouble with her inner organs, and then I saw that it looked like her leg had been amputated. I gulped. How could I start the reading by saying, "I see someone with their leg amputated—your grandmother, perhaps?" It seemed very risky. Even if my intuitive readings are focused on handling life, no intuitive reader wants to be far off the mark. But I had to trust this, so I continued to explore the drawing.

As this was really the first time I used an intuitive stream drawing in a reading, it was simpler in form and not as detailed as others that followed. The drawings evolved as I did, so they take new forms and have become more detailed as I've continued to use and understand them.

Draw with Emotion: This is the drawing (Figure 32) and this is how I saw the drawing when I gazed at it (see Figure 33; see insert for color version):

Gaze: As I gazed at this drawing, all the lines and shapes began to take form. I saw people in it. The first thing I saw (in the upper right area) resembled a grandmother, possibly in the hospital. It looked like tubes or wires were attached to her chest and

Figure 32.
Case Study: Love and Grief—Grandmother.

under her mouth. As I explained, the figure was missing a leg. I could not ignore that visual perception. Under her, I saw what might have been another hospitalized person, with a bandage on their foot, and a third person (a male, in my mind).

Trust Your Words: I trusted what came to me, even though it felt a little risky. I didn't know if what I perceived could be correct, but I decided that since the feelings I was having were so genuine, I should go with it.

I turned my attention to the image beneath the grandmother with the amputated leg. The bottom figure looked as if it had been struck down and killed. The intuitive stream drawing began to shift into an entirely different scene (see Figure 34). The more I gazed at it, the more I connected with this other perspective. Visually, I saw

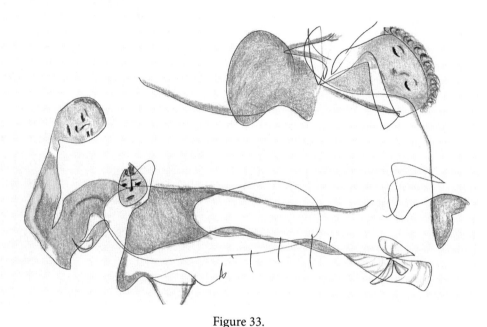

Figure 33.
Case Study: Love and Grief—Grandmother, colored in.

this figure as male (even though there was no particular reason for me to see it as male), but that is what came to mind. Perhaps I had a prejudice about aggression and fighting, connecting that with male behavior. (Becoming more conscious of my own associations also helps me examine my perceptions and question them so I can grow in my view of the world. I encourage you to accept what comes to mind. Do not judge yourself. Make note of your perceptions so you can see them for what they are and adjust them. You have gained knowledge and enhanced your perceptions—adding new to the old or even tossing away old ideas that do not serve you or others. For this exploration, though, it is important to accept and trust what comes without blocking it).

This drawing was beginning to show me many dimensions of thought. Where at first I had seen a grandmother with an amputated leg, I now saw this shape take on the

Figure 34.
Case Study: Love and Grief—Attacker.

look of an aggressive attacker leaning over a fallen person who had been struck down forcibly (see Figure 35; see insert for color version). I continued to gaze at the drawing.

I thought the figure who had fallen had been killed in some kind of violent way. There was even another figure close to him below, hovering over his head, in grief or shock (see Figure 36; see insert for color version). I felt that someone must have witnessed the figure's death, as the drawing indicated he was not alone on the ground. He seemed to have wounds: note the bandage-like formation on the right foot, which to me signified healing a wound, or a wound itself. I thought the aggressor was possibly holding a knife or other sharp object.

As I looked at what I had created with my eyes closed, and what I was seeing when I gazed at the drawing, I became excited. However, I also tried to convince myself that this could not be: how could one person have a grandmother who had

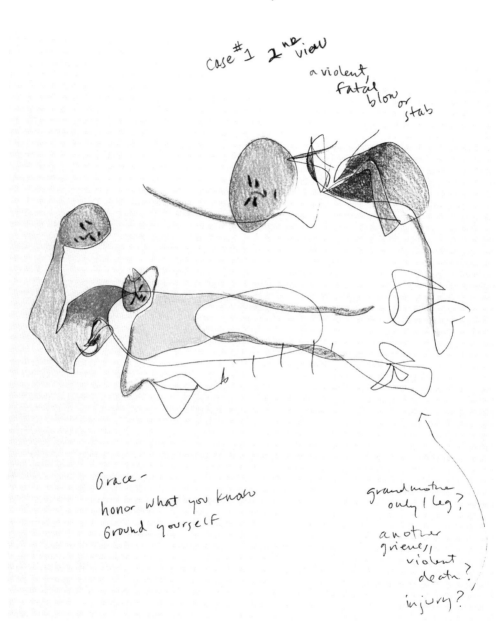

Case #1 2nd view

a violent, fatal blow or stab

Grace—
honor what you know
Ground yourself

grandmother only 1 leg?

another grievous violent death? injury?

Figure 35.

Case Study: Love and Grief—Attacker, colored in.

a leg amputated and then also know someone personally who was killed in a violent way? It seemed like a lot for any one person to go through. Not impossible, but a *lot*. This imagery was specific enough to be very important if the drawing and my interpretation was correct. I asked myself if this could be true. Could the drawing truly be showing me important experiences in this client's life, or the experiences of people she knew and loved? Could I trust my inner thoughts and words as they came to me?

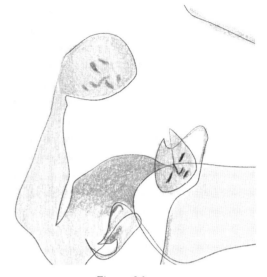

Figure 36.
Case Study: Love and Grief—Attacker, detail (witness to the attack).

I was trying my best to dodge the intuitive signs (the visual information in the drawing), since the information arrived from what would ordinarily be considered random marks with no meaning. But when the phone rang a few minutes later and the reading began, I put my neck out and told her I had created an intuitive stream drawing for her and said that I would tell her what came up in it. I said, "I see someone close to you who has had a leg amputated." Her answer: "Yes, when my grandmother was in the hospital, they cut her leg off."

Right then and there, I knew that this was the way I needed to approach intuitive readings. At the very least, it was well worth investigating as a promising intuitive method. I had felt urged to do this drawing, and something about intuition was being communicated with me in the unfolding of my interpretation.

So when the client confirmed that she had known an older man who had been killed when he tried to break up a bar fight, I felt again the surge of relief and amazement—somehow, in some way, my first attempt at an "intuitive stream drawing" proved fruitful.

During my first spontaneous attempt at intuitively creating a drawing to support a client, I had not yet developed the "four directions" method (turning the drawing four ways to increase the visual-intuitive viewpoints). This intuitive stream drawing reading only includes one time line and one chakra chart. But for the purpose of helping you develop visual-intuitive play, I encourage you to look at the drawing to see what you see in it. I encourage you to refer to the first black-and-white printing of this image (Figure 32) at the beginning of this section, and turn it four ways to see how the shapes and lines speak to you! You may see what I saw, plus many other things I did not recognize. I share with you both the artistic vision of describing my intuitive impressions of the shapes and lines as well as the analytical process I use with clients daily, in the hope that you'll develop your own unique approach.

Case Study Continued: Chakra Chart View

To gain a new perspective on this drawing, I turned it ninety degrees to see what I could find (this practice developed into the "chakra chart" view). This angle of the drawing (see Figure 37; see insert for color version) showed me what felt like a mother with child. The mother seemed to be wearing an apron, which made me think perhaps this represented the client's mother; an internal, maternal self; or learning to embrace or cope with traditional roles (such as motherhood and housekeeping).

When I focused exclusively on the maternal figure, she appeared to be possibly loosening the apron ties (breaking free of traditional female roles and expectations, perhaps). She had at her feet (root chakra) a champagne bottle tied with a red bow. This felt to me that she either deserved a reward or had one coming: she deserved to be celebrated. Also, there was an image that reminded me of a heart-shaped helium balloon with a string attached. This had deflated and floated below her feet to the ground, signifying lost love or disappointment in love. Another strong visual reference for me was that the woman looked like a figure from a Marc Chagall painting, with a theme of love and richness in intimate, spiritually evolving relationships.

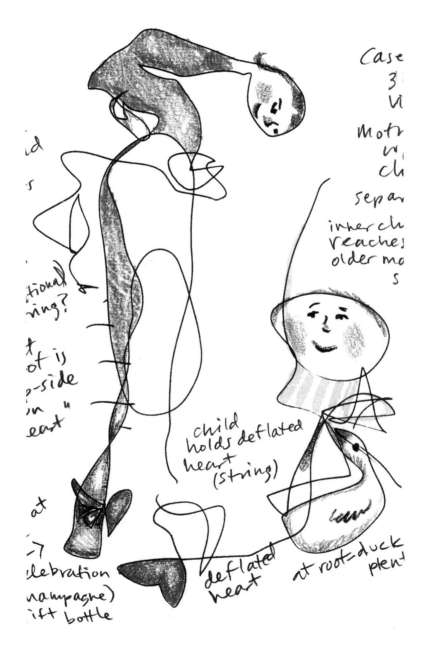

Figure 37.
Case Study: Love and Grief—chakra chart, detail (apron strings).

Focusing now on the image of the child (see Figure 38; see insert for color version) reaching up to the mother. This would indicate the client as a child, her inner child, or a literal child of her own. The child reached up in a gesture of trust that the parent will respond. At the child's feet (root chakra), I saw a duck shape, signifying for me "having plenty" as well as an association with nursery rhymes. The child seemed to hold the "heartstring," the sign of deflated love residing at the mother's feet.

Again, not all of the viewpoints of this intuitive stream drawing (second time line and chakra chart readings) are included here, but gaze at the image yourself. Turn it and see what you see!

Drawing Conclusions

Visual-intuitive suggestion in intuitive stream drawings is strong. There are many ways to see into them. Taking your time to gaze is part of the fascination: each time you look at lines and forms and how they come together, you may perceive another visual-intuitive message. As you begin to read for yourself and others, remember that each intuitive stream drawing reading has its four directions. You can zero in on multiple images in each view. This means that the stream drawing will offer you new imagery, insights, and ways to understand and comprehend its messages.

Doing intuitive stream drawing readings in honor of another person gives you an opportunity to experience how another person's life feels, or how episodes of life bring a world of feeling along with them. Enjoy each unique intuitive stream drawing reading: by using your perception in pursuit of deeper understanding, healing and enlightenment can take place in unexpected and delightful ways.

Figure 38.
Case Study: Love and Grief—chakra chart, detail (child).

11

Drawing as a Pathway to Intuitive Discoveries at Home and Abroad

We can learn to use our intuition and empathic sensing to develop a keener idea of what we love and what we don't; what situations are optimal for our growth, and which ones are destructive for us. We can sift our way through life's ups and downs (and have fun doing it) when we use our logic along with intuitive intelligence. We use all the knowledge we have within us to make our choices and solve our problems. At home, school, work, and in our community at large, we can thrive if we trust that our intuition will guide us. We discover ourselves and celebrate the development of those around us. Since drawing is one way to keep the intuitive flow coming, we can figure out ways to use drawing and integrate it into our lives.

Drawing More at Home

Drawing is fun and provides a release of tension. It is another way to communicate that brings out the playfulness in people who live together. In many ways, stream drawing is a personal, introverted exercise. But try it as a lighthearted, intuitive game with family members. You might ask if anyone has a question or a concern (as in the style of Henry Reed's Dream Helper Ceremony). Without knowing the concern, the rest of the family stream draws for answers to the subject's question. Once the stream drawings are done, a discussion follows: the *Discover and Connect* phase. Sharing the imagery and its possible meanings may provide unexpected insights and solutions. Bonding in this way is nice, because the family member acting as the subject may also *not* wish to share her question or concern; she may choose to just listen to the others' intuitive messages. A teenager trying to gain independence, for example, may feel supported and emotionally connected to the family while also keeping a sense of distance.

Also, stream drawing together for questions that are not so serious but mysterious is really fun. You can ask questions like "Are UFOs really real?" "What do you think I'll be when I grow up?" or "Where will I live when I grow up?" A parent may ask, "Where should we go when we retire?"

Questions that seem lighthearted at first may actually be serious, after all. For example, a mother had trouble sleeping. Nothing seemed to help. A stream drawing done by her sister about the issue led them to discuss the subject's husband. He took up most of the room in the bed, snored, and was causing her to wake up. A can of soda was visible in the stream drawing, so they talked about cutting out caffeine. There was also a dog in the drawing. The subject said that her dog kept her awake by moving around at night. These factors all exacerbated her sleep issue. The stream drawing offered her ways to solve the problem (get a bigger bed, keep the dog in a separate room, and so forth).

In general, families are so busy these days that suggesting they will have time to sit around a table and stream draw to music or for fun may seem unrealistic. But what would happen if the choice to draw was always available, and you had supplies ready and an open attitude? Consider dedicating five minutes after dinner to stream draw together—right before (or during, or in place of) dessert.

Some families and groups of friends are intrigued by the paranormal and like to play psychic games, have discussions about ghosts, and so on. Doing intuitive stream drawing readings to seek answers to little mysteries may be appealing. Whatever your interest is, stream drawing can be a part of it.

There are ways to make intuitive streaming, drawing, and seeing intuitively a natural part of your life at home. Below are some ideas, and you may already have many of your own.

Dream Dragon

While teaching young children, I learned that one of the best and most creative ways of helping children who are dealing with heavily emotional and visual dream content was the "Dream Dragon." The dragon was a sculpture in the hallway of the Atrium School, where I taught in Boston. The founder of the school, Virginia Kahn, was very sensitive to how dreams influence children and their emotional and psychological well-being. Each morning at school, any child who had a troubling dream could draw and write about it, and drop it in the Dream Dragon's mouth at the end of the hallway. This was a brilliant solution. It gave the children the same understanding my father had given me: it is okay to dream, and you can do something about it. The Dream Dragon had an added benefit of reminding the children that their teachers understood how dreams have the power to follow you—you don't have to keep silent about them. There is a private and creative outlet for processing them.

The Mural Wall

There is usually no stopping very young kids from drawing on walls, on themselves, anywhere! To welcome this natural and empowering instinct, there are ways to encourage it rather than discourage it. One way is to have a chalkboard-painted wall, or to designate one wall in your house as the "mural wall." After the space gets filled with in-house kiddie graffiti, you can photograph the wall. Then, clean and repaint it for a fresh start. Having boundaries and rules about drawing is reasonable: "Draw on this wall, not that one." Everyone can enjoy creative expression as a part of home life.

Visual-Intuitive Scavenger Hunt

Since drawing involves seeing intuitively and using a visual-intuitive language, there are ways to encourage your vision. Seeing with artistic, empathic vision—feeling connected to your surroundings—can help you set up scavenger hunts based on visual stimuli. Instead of going out to find objects, you can search for all the faces in rocks and trees, or the alphabet letters in their names, for example. This is fun and connects us with our surroundings in a more intuitive way. In nature, our neighborhoods, fences, and building exteriors we see things we may have missed before. If tree roots come together in a *Y* shape, for example, and that letter is in a child's name, he can "collect" it with a photograph, sketch, or simply by showing it to others, along with all the other letters in his name. A tire wheel may be the letter *O*; a mailbox looks like a lowercase *n*, and so on. A rock may have a smiling face. A house's half-open window becomes a winking eye. A dear friend of mine has five framed photographs on her kitchen wall; each one is a "found" letter of the alphabet, spelling the family surname. It is delightful. Scavenging for letters that spell out a child's name or initials, framing, and hanging them on the wall is a lot of fun, too.

Multimedia: Drawing in the TV Room

Computer games seem to take children's complete attention these days, and they watch television as well. All in all, it seems like way too much screen time—but maybe it is possible to make drawing a part of it. Keep a pad of paper and pencils or markers in your TV room. Chances are, kids will draw while they watch TV, which means they'll be creating a running narrative in their minds that is rooted in their own imagination. They'll be able to use drawing to calm down and center themselves, when otherwise they might just be sitting motionless in front of the television. Not all children will choose to draw, but if the adults in the house draw "little streamers" also called stream drawings (see Figure 39; see insert for color version), while watching, it may teach how the creative mind does not have to be shut off; we do not have to surrender to a

Figure 39.
Little streamers.

semihypnotic state, staring at a screen. Just having art supplies (especially paper and nice pencils) next to the TV makes a point.

Ideals and Living an Intuitive Career Life

I have a client who works in the financial district, a corporate environment. She and her boss start each day with a conversation about intuition. They talk about dreams or other impressions from life. They post images at their desks that remind them of their creative spirits. It seems like a rare gift that they have found this way to bond in the corporate world. They embrace a meditative, intuitive approach in a traditionally competitive environment. Meditation in other forms has found its way into institutions in the form of yoga, for example (offered in the workplace to employees). Since not being in the "fight or flight" mode has been proven to help people use as much brain power as possible, this seems like a necessity: a way to work that is far more beneficial.

Not being comfortable enough at work to be intuitive and get creative is a common problem. We forget what truly matters to us as we focus more on outside demands. It is easy to plod along carrying out responsibilities, forgetting that we can develop our lives according to our inner sense of self and our truest ideals. What we feel—from the inside out—is worthy and meaningful. Those ideals can be lost as we get busy building a foundation for life in practical ways (maintaining a job or home). We forget that this gift, our ability to access and experience our ideals, is in our very hands. As a form of meditation, drawing may begin with no particular goal or intention; still, the act of stream drawing (especially if done frequently) can loosen up the layers of bedrock inside. We begin to feel good. Eventually, we connect the practice of drawing with feeling good. It puts us in a place we'd like to visit more often. We grasp what we know or believe will make us happy. From that point, we can stream draw to figure out how to build a foundation for a new life—for the spirit of life, creative abundance, and well-being.

Recently, one of my clients said he was looking to figure out what his life purpose was. He was in his forties. His parents had told him all his life to get a "practical" job, which was a good piece of advice. Being self-sufficient and practical meant he would not only survive, he would have all his needs met. But he had no sense of true purpose. He was not feeling fulfilled in his life. He got a degree in something that did not interest him, and his job bored him. He was not being nurtured at all in his waking hours. He was not in touch with the ideals or dreams he once had for his life. In fact, he had no idea what those dreams were anymore. My meditation prior to his session showed that he was ready to stop doing "hard labor" and reawaken his sense of passion for life. In the stream drawing I did for him, there was an area of lines and shapes that looked like a person working in a rice paddy. I took this to mean hard, repetitive, uncreative work for this client. During the meditation, I felt the pain of the worker's burden. Then, when the session began, I asked him about this particular image and message. He said the one thing he wanted was to figure out what he loved. Nobody could tell him but himself, though. He had accepted a laborious life of struggle in a virtual rice paddy and needed to rediscover his ideals and love for life. He had inherited his parents' memories of suffering in poverty and carried them (along with their advice about practical work) without letting go; yet he wanted intensely to try a new concept for his own life. We talked about stream drawing as a way for him to begin to feel again, especially to feel compassion for himself. Stream drawing would allow him to "just be," with the intention of listening inward and drawing out the self-knowledge he wanted. He could do this at any time of day, on short breaks or after work. Immediately, he could start being more intuitive; he could begin sensing and responding to the emotions within him that were shut off when he focused on the practical issues of life.

Many clients mention their stresses at work, especially frustrating relationships with coworkers. One of the best ways to get a new perspective on someone (such as coworker or boss who presents difficulty) is to stream draw in honor of them. If you can draw with emotion—not just how you feel, but also what makes them tick and how they feel—there is relief in that. You may get enough distance to realize that people are influenced by all kinds of life situations. Understanding or getting the slightest view of those influences may be helpful. It gives you emotional distance and shifts you from a reactionary mode to reflectiveness. The stream drawing interpretations also help you understand yourself better; this allows you to get a bird's-eye view of your own emotions. Then, you stop being impulsive in your behavior. You have the choice to react with a sense of calmness, knowledge, and composure, rather than automatic defensiveness.

Doing intuitive stream drawing readings for yourself to ask for guidance in all work situations also gives you a chance to see why you feel a certain way at work, and how to make things better. But getting that serenity is the most important thing—to draw for the purpose of separating yourself from the situation, exploring difficult dynamics, and keeping destructive emotional impulses and responses out of the picture. This practice leaves you more conscious and aware and ready to choose to respond in a way you think is best.

Stream drawing could be tried to intuit creative solutions at work, too. If you are supposed to brainstorm, use intuitive stream drawing to relax and get the channels flowing. Physically, getting into that zone is easy once you start drawing. Then, the mind (ideas) and heart (inspiration and desire to find a solution) get flowing, too. If you get comfortable with the stream drawing method and want to share it with others at work, maybe having a stream drawing meet-up now and then would be not only fun but liberating and possibly helpful. This is the most optimal disposition. People are productive and enthusiastic when they feel expressive and in a creative flow. As you try this on your own, you might develop unique, specific methods for using stream drawing for your particular needs. You might even stream yourself into your next job—your dream job.

Stream Drawing in Your Community

Once a year, my community devotes an entire month to drawing. Local businesses and artists partner to draw on the windows on Main Street. The arts center and library provide exciting and fun drawing workshops—I do one at the library! It is a happy, lively time. Drawing, that thing that everyone can do in one way or another, becomes the link. It is an inclusive, interesting, productive, and joyous activity.

Stream drawing can bring communities together to enjoy, bond, and be playful together. At local gatherings, fundraisers, or meetings, stream drawing can be part of the action. People love to see drawing in community events (like face painting or funny character portraits), but it seems like only people who are "good at art" do the drawing, while everyone else watches. But what if everyone was invited? There are ways to draw that are both enjoyable and available to everyone.

I think that stream drawing's healing and expressive nature is ideal for college campuses (as I have done with students and faculty) and support groups. People may struggle to find ways to express their fears and worries, and drawing provides this outlet. The steps of stream drawing help us connect outward and relate our personal struggles. When everyone is focusing on a drawing (rather than on a person who is having a hard time), discussions may flow more easily and feel less emotionally risky. A drawing can remind us how truly connected we are to one another, and feeling that connection provides security and support.

In every culture, drawing is a common language all humans share. We are born mark makers. Hopefully, our culture will shift from thinking of drawing as a skill of rendering that only a few people develop (while the rest look on) to seeing drawing as a process and experience based on creative willpower that is worth doing beyond childhood. Stream drawing is inclusive and finds value in all of us. It is ready to find a place in our hands, friendships, families, workplaces, and communities.

Everyone at the Easel

Ever since I began doing gesture drawing workshops at schools, in libraries, and at museums more than twenty years ago, I realized how this exercise can increase mindfulness and empathy in learners. As an artist, intuitive reader, and former teacher, it is one of the most rewarding and exciting things I do with groups. Emotional intelligence enriches a person's experience in life; it is part of developing well as an individual, especially in terms of living an intuitive life. We don't learn well when we're afraid or uncomfortable, and so much constructive cooperation is dashed when schoolchildren are taught to switch off their personal feelings and their capacity to empathize with others. Competition and fear do not always bring out the best in us, so we need to reinforce love and respect in order to coexist. Love (feeling genuine appreciation and affection for another person) and respect (to value another person

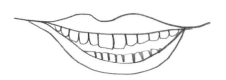

and hold her in high regard) are present when we take time to get in touch with our emotions and understand that others also have feelings and deserve acknowledgment. As I said earlier in this book, competition can be healthy, but it can also create a win-or-lose dynamic. In this scenario, the relaxation required for full brain function is missing. "Fight or flight" survival mode is activated, while the intuitive, emotional, and creative side of the brain is shut down. But when we acknowledge our emotions and try to cooperate instead of competing, creativity flows and empathy grows. Too much competition encourages us to compare ourselves to others, which means we look *outside of ourselves* to determine who we are. Being intuitive is about *going inward* to discover who we are based on our experiences, emotions, thoughts, desires, and actions. We can see how we are connected to others who are like us. Having empathy begins with our own ability to acknowledge how we feel as we extend the same compassion to others. It means realizing that other people are not so different from us: we do not have to struggle against one another.

Drawing with passion and a feeling of well-being opens us up to our empathic potential. This potential needs to be nourished in order to cooperate, understand, and function well with others. When I started using a particular method of gesture drawing known as "blind contour" drawing with schoolchildren—to encourage intuitive exploration—it was easy to see that each child had an original, powerful urge to make marks.

For this exercise, I set up an easel with a large pad of newsprint as the focal point of the room. The person at the easel is to stand comfortably, holding a soft piece of vine charcoal. The charcoal is easy to wipe away—this is about creating the mark with empathy, allowing the hand to express the feeling while drawing the contour shape of the subject. The group is asked to imagine how it would feel to be up there in front of everyone, daring to draw, and risking an injury to their self-esteem. Group members support the person in the middle. They are not to laugh or make fun of the drawing—only enjoy it and encourage the mark maker, no matter how the drawing comes out. The purpose of the exercise is not to create a particular kind of drawing; rather, it is to represent the emotional, intuitive intelligence of the mark maker at the easel.

The mark maker is to gaze at another person—the person who is posing—and hold that gaze, feeling how it would be to "stand in another person's moccasins"— while drawing the contour of the poser/subject. Without looking at the paper, she draws a contour of the subject using large, free, and loose motions of the arm. The person posing could make an emotive gesture of some kind, such as hunching over in exhaustion or reaching up in surprise. The witnesses count to twenty in a whisper as the mark maker draws.

The mark maker is encouraged to draw large and fast, rather than small and slow. If a person draws small and slow in this exercise, she will usually begin to feel self-doubt, take her eyes off the subject, and look at the paper to "correct" what is "wrong" about the drawing. When this happens, the empathic and intuitive process is frozen. Fear reigns. The mark maker at the easel begins to stare at the paper and feel isolated from the group. She stops engaging with the subject or herself. In her effort to "draw correctly," small details such as tiny eyelashes and clothing become the focus; the mark maker begins to fuss. She loses her focus on the overall emotional gesture of the subject.

If this happens, the group encourages the mark maker to back away from those fears. They remind her that any mark made while gazing at the subject is absolutely wonderful and good. With care and verbal and emotional support from the group, the mark maker draws without self-doubt; she gets to experience self-acceptance in front of the group.

Since there is no "correct" way to draw in this intuitive exercise, there is no need for self-doubt. When the mark maker at the easel trusts herself and feels support from the group, she can truly empathize with the subject. She can draw with authentic, energetic intent. Suddenly, making marks based on her respectful regard of another person (the subject) is translated into self-empowerment and empathy. The group gets to feel the benefits of their generosity toward the mark maker. Ideally, this exercise is repeated within this group until everyone has had a chance to make marks based on their empathy toward a subject (many can volunteer to pose). After the workshop ends, the easel is not put away but set up somewhere in the school, with plenty of newsprint and charcoal so that the children can continue to draw

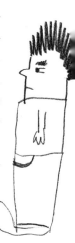

and practice this intuitive exercise. This drawing exercise always generates sponta-neous appreciation and excitement; I am sure that is due in part to the message that our feelings are valued, and therefore important. So is the essence of the marks we make, especially those that represent our esteem for other human beings. I think another reason people respond enthusiastically to this exercise is because we know we have empathic, intuitive intelligence. Any experience in life that allows us to use this intelligence, especially as members of a group, resonates as meaningful. It gives us well-being.

This drawing exercise is not new to artists. It is popular in studios where models pose while artists practice "blind contours." This is also known as "gesture drawing," drawing without looking at the paper, studying the model's gestures, and releasing the potential to self-edit. Using a continuous charcoal line and working with quick-ness strengthens the hand–brain connection. Once an artist has confidence and discipline, drawing more slowly is helpful to study the contour and volume of the model. The artist can practice drawing what is actually happening, as opposed to what he may assume is happening. This is a common practice, especially for figura-tive artists, who translate intuitive intelligence into expressive works with drawing, painting, and sculpture. What makes it exciting and meaningful to do in schools, in regular classrooms, is that it unlocks a child's original, innate, and instinctive impulse to be expressive. Children inherently know how to intuit with compassion. They can practice using an open heart to feel not just what someone experiences in their physical gestures, but what that person feels on many levels—including the need to be accepted and valued as a unique individual within the group. This creates a healthy learning environment: a humanistic, thoughtful, and inclusive atmosphere in which intuitive intelligence is acknowledged and validated.

The marks we make come from our internal response system as our senses work together to collect information and react to it. If we expect our marks to be used only to determine our worth and "success" as individuals, we shut down our empathy and intuition. We are scared into competing, trying to prove we are capable of success, and ranking each other accordingly. How different it is when we make marks to honor the intrinsic worth of others, while embodying self-trust and compassion.

Drawing out of intuitive intelligence is not difficult, simply because it is our nature to intuit. We enjoy the thrill of making marks; it is our birthright. Without having to think about it, we intuitively respond to our environment. The marks we make say we're alive. We think, we feel, and we are unique. There is no way to truly destroy the intuitive wellspring within us, but our society can do a pretty good job stunting it. For me, drawing to encourage intuitive intelligence is the core of my life as an artist, teacher, and intuitive reader and healer. We're all creators and healers in our own right, and I believe it starts with the first marks we make.

Some Drawing Games

Mystery Draw

In this game, players take turns choosing from a stack of cards, each one with a descriptive word on it, such as "squiggly" or "straight" or "jagged." If the children are young, an adult helper can read the word with them, whispering it in their ear. Nobody else knows the word but the child who picked the card. He runs to the center of the room (where some drawing paper is laid out), and draws the line as described. The next player chooses a word and connects his line with the one that has already been drawn, or starts a new one somewhere else on the paper.

A variation on this is to take a piece of paper and fold it four times. The first person draws a head at the top of the page—nobody else gets to see it. Folding the paper to hide the head, this player passes the paper to the next person, who draws the neck, arms and torso. He folds the paper again to cover the head and torso sections. The next person draws the legs, and so forth, down to the feet. When the players unfold the paper, it is really fun to see how the "portrait" comes out, with the head, torso, legs, and feet each drawn by different people, not knowing what the others have drawn.

Nouns and Adjectives

In this game, there are two stacks of cards. One stack has nouns written on each card (such as "chair" or "duck"). The other stack is all adjectives ("golden" or "angry"). The players choose one card from each stack and put the two cards together, making a drawing of the result. Here's an example of one possible outcome: a child chose from the noun stack and got the word "bike." When he chose from the adjective stack he got the word "hungry." This child drew a bike that looked like an alligator. The spokes were teeth and the handlebars became like horns. The bike was trying to eat a person who was running away.

Drawing Conclusions

In this chapter, there are ideas for using a visual-intuitive approach to life with others, at home and in the community. Some of these exercises come from the drawing workshop I've done for years, and are extremely important to me as an artist and an intuitive reader. Others mentioned in this last chapter are meant to be little brainstorms—ways to incorporate drawing and to see intuitively in your daily life. From playing visual games to drawing dreams to put in the dragon's mouth, there are many opportunities to enhance and support intuitive sensing, feeling, and seeing throughout your day. The suggestions in this chapter are meant to kick-start you to develop your own ideas. Taking your intuition to work or school and reinforcing it at home through drawing can start with small gestures, which may expand, giving unexpected and delightful results. You're on your way discovering the extraordinary, building your creativity, and relating to other people in playful ways in the world around you.

This interactive guidebook has taken you on an intuitive journey to discover and reclaim your true essence: that of the mark maker. Drawing satisfies at the deepest level, as your perceptions are accompanied by the instinct to make an impression. You have explored the way stream-of-consciousness drawing centers us, allowing the unconscious and the conscious mind to relate harmoniously. You have discovered that through drawing, you can find meaning on your own terms and express your perceptions. You have seen how drawing connects you to the world from the inside out, with compassion, empathy, and insight.

With practice, you have developed an expectation that you can learn from your imaginative, emotional, and powerful stream drawings. You can also celebrate others

in their creative expression through drawing. Intuitive stream drawings can tell you who you are as you draw yourself into being each moment. By using drawing as an intuitive way to feel and gather knowledge, you can see that it connects you to other people in profound, fundamental ways.

Just as a line starts in one place and ends in another, humans grow through time and life experiences. We make choices with some measure of intention; we try to go in the direction we wish our lives to take. Our perception of ourselves is influenced by many factors as we move through time and space, expressing, creating, and communicating what we see, feel, and believe.

That blank page of opportunity we have at birth is marked—moment by moment—with the many strokes of our desires, wishes and intentions, hopes, and suffering. No wonder drawing is universal! We knew from the moment we arrived that we were born mark makers.

Acknowledgments

I would like to thank Lisa Hagan of Lisa Hagan Literary (formerly of Paraview), my valiant agent, who championed this book on intuitive mark making from the beginning. I also thank my wonderful and inspiring mentors, Dr. Laurie Nadel, PhD, and Dr. Eldon Taylor, PhD, for their time, generosity, and brilliance. I thank Anna Noak, my editor at Beyond Words, for connecting with the purpose, vision, and spirit in this book. And my husband, Simon Boughton, for his encouragement and support, always.

Duude....

Index of Exercises

Try It! Experiment with Line Gradation   14

Try It! Frozen Pond Exercise   17

Try It! Use Your Opposite Hand   19

Try It! Get a Sense   31

Try It! Gaze for Yourself   35

Try It! Drops in the Ocean: Multiple Lines Creating One Whole Form   36

Try It! See the Personality of Shapes   38

Try It! Perceiving Lines and Shapes as Universal Messengers   43

Try It! Change Agents: Evocative Arrangements of Line and Shape   49

Try It! Create Your Own Memory Drawing   57

Try It! Happy Memory Drawing   60

Try It! Angry Memory Drawing   62

Try It! Sad Memory Drawing   64

Try It! Nervous Memory Drawing   66

Try It! Put It All Together   68

Try It! Stream Draw with Emotion   74

Try It! Create a Streaming and Dreaming Drawing   92

Try It! Conduct a Streaming and Dreaming Experiment   96

Try It! Stream Drawing and Problem Solving   131

Try It! Stream Draw for a Partner   145

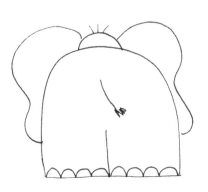

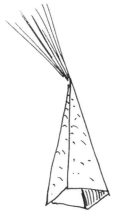

Index of Figures

Figure 1. My drawing of Buddy-Randy and his family on a
book's endpapers. xvi

Figure 2. Line gradation experiment. 16

Figure 3. Frozen pond drawing exercise. 18

Figure 4. Sensory lines. 31

Figure 5. Line drawing comparison, part one. 33

Figure 6. Line drawing comparison, part two. 34

Figure 7. Line drawing comparison, part three. 36

Figure 8. Line drawing comparison of many lines together. 37

Figure 9. A line and shape together. 39

Figure 10. Rectangle and oval comparison. 41

Figure 11. Triangle comparison. 42

Figure 12. Line and square shape together.   44

Figure 13. Smiley face, frowny face.   45

Figure 14. Smiley brow.   46

Figure 15. Line with small oval as shut eye and teardrop.   48

Figure 16. Line and small oval, turned.   49

Figure 17. Brianna's happy memory drawing.   59

Figure 18. Passive line.   77

Figure 19. Passive line with my notations.   78

Figure 20a. Original drawing.   95

Figure 20b. My stream drawing of a person falling off a horse.   95

Figure 21. The four directions.   107

Figure 22. First time line.   115

Figure 23. First time line, colored in.   116

Figure 24. First chakra chart.   118

Figure 25. First chakra chart, colored in.   119

Figure 26. Second time line.   120

Figure 27. Second time line, colored in.   121

Figure 28. Second chakra chart.   123

Figure 29. Second chakra chart, colored in.   124

Figure 30. An image of sharp broken glass in an intuitive
            stream drawing reading.   129

Figure 31. An image of a car crash in an intuitive stream drawing reading.   139

Figure 32. Case Study: Love and Grief—Grandmother.   149

Figure 33. Case Study: Love and Grief—Grandmother, colored in.   150

Figure 34. Case Study: Love and Grief—Attacker.   151

Figure 35. Case Study: Love and Grief—Attacker, colored in.   152

Figure 36. Case Study: Love and Grief—Attacker, detail
    (witness to the attack).   153

Figure 37. Case Study: Love and Grief—chakra chart, detail (apron strings).   155

Figure 38. Case Study: Love and Grief—chakra chart, detail (child).   157

Figure 39. Little streamers.   162

A Quick Look at Visual-Intuitive Meanings

By sharing out loud how the visual imagery in an intuitive stream drawing reading conjures meanings based on personal experiences, no matter how odd they may feel or seem at the time, the subject has a chance to connect your interpretations to something she may not have seen without your empathic sharing. Interpretations are modes of empathy and are the focus of intuitive stream drawing readings because by sharing what the imagery means to you personally, you open the door to insights for the subject and yourself.

In most intuitive or psychic readings, the subject remains silent as the reader expresses what comes. When the reading is good, much of what the intuitive reader says resonates in some way with the subject. Sometimes my interpretations don't seem to mean a thing for the subject until well after the reading is over, but usually both of us know when there is good flow and a sense of revelation.

Intuitive stream drawing interpretation is done in the spirit of sharing what comes to mind for the intuitive stream drawer and seeing if it holds meaning for the subject, so nobody loses. Most likely, the subject will connect well with what you share, but you aren't a bad reader if the subject does not connect right away with all of your interpretations. Often a client will contact me after a reading to say that they suddenly realized what something in his or her intuitive stream drawing meant, though they didn't understand it at the time. Also, since I promise to say what I see, I trust that it is there for a reason. I may ask to reflect on an image with the subject for a bit to see other ways of perceiving it or to understand the meaning, which may not be obvious right away. So don't let it crush your spirit or scare you away from continuing to share what you draw and what you see, even if the meaning takes time to figure out. You have to believe in the process and enjoy what it offers. If the subject is open-minded and open-hearted, the conversation that may follow allows the subject to look at situations in a new way. It can be a most compelling and healing way to be enlightened and empowered.

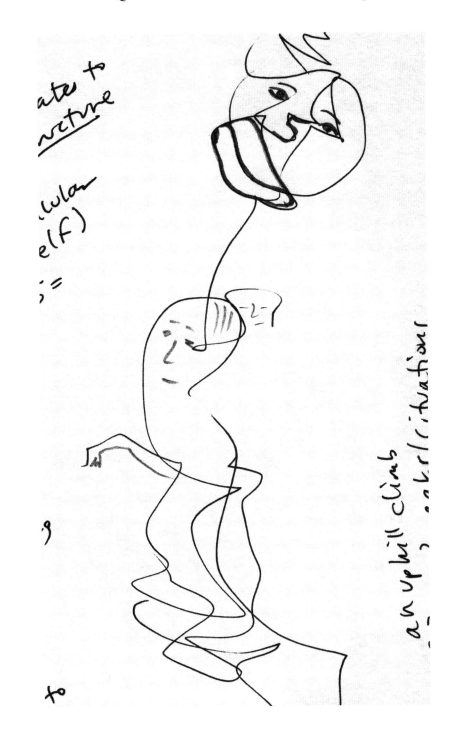

Kiss of Acceptance and Mobility

In this intuitive stream drawing reading, at the top of the first chakra chart I saw a circular head shape, and at the bottom left, huge lips. What would lips signify for you? For me, lips in an intuitive stream drawing represent "the kiss of acceptance": wanting to be loved and desired, especially in a romantic way. Above that I saw a number 5. Can you also find it? What does the number 5 remind you of or bring to mind? For me, it stands for mobility and change. It looks like a chariot or even a wheelchair to me. Change may be something we champion (determination), or something we resist (conflict), but when I see the number 5, change of some kind is in the air. So I put those two concepts together—wanting to be desired romantically and change. There is potential conflict but positive mobility through the situation, since the number 5 is facing forward, moving into the future. (The client wanted a platonic relationship to blossom into romance before she and her friend graduated from college.)

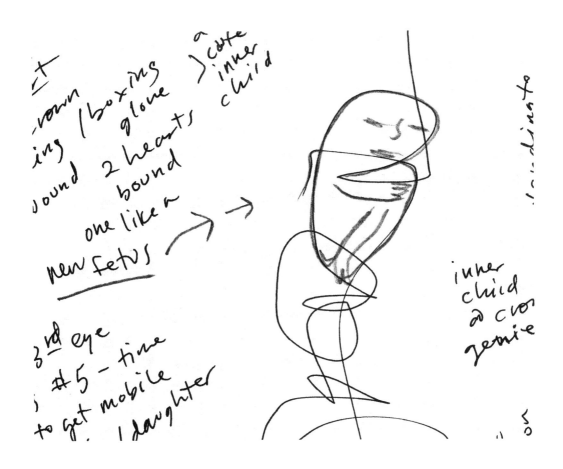

t

vorm

ing / boxing
       glove

a cute
inner
child

ound 2 hearts
           bound

one like a

new fetus → →

l coudinato

inner
child
a cros
gemie

3rd eye
: #5 - time
to get mobile
         . l daughter

5

Loss and New Life

In this image, I saw a fetus at the crown chakra. Does a fetus bring up any thoughts, feelings, or memories for you? For me, a fetus may signify new beginnings and be purely symbolic of the early stages of a new experience, but it can also be literal. In this case, it was literal in two ways: the client had suffered a miscarriage and I felt she longed for (and might receive) a new child in the near future. It felt promising and poignant when I gazed at it, and its location in the crown chakra gave me hope (the crown chakra having to do with divine purpose and connection).

Sword of Courage

What would a sword image mean to you in a drawing? For me here, there was a sharp object, and "sword" came to mind above any other thing such as "glass" or "razor." It just wanted to be a sword. It even had a little knight's shield next to it (can you see it?). That part of the intuitive stream drawing was making a Z stroke, so I thought of Zorro, which I associate with courage and confidence. After sharing this, I learned that this client had recently used her own personal "Zorro sword" at work by taking a risk and voicing her opinion about something that involved her integrity. She asserted herself bravely. The sword image for her was a powerful confirmation that she had done the right thing, or at least an acknowledgment of what the scenario felt like to her.

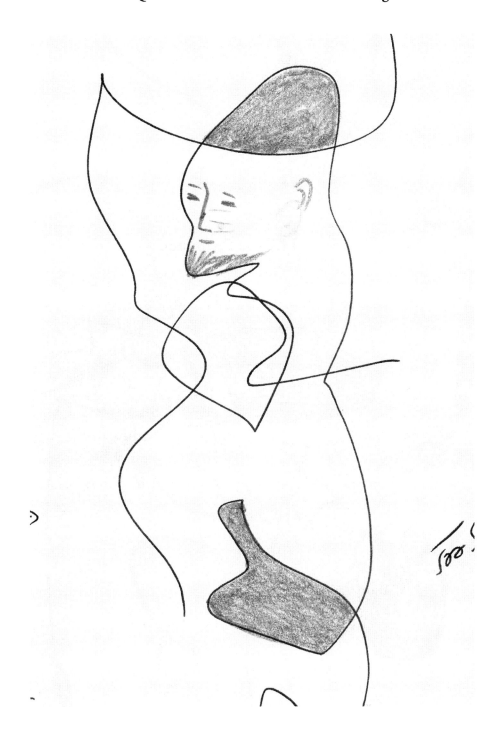

The Rabbi and the Spade

I meditated by drawing before a phone appointment with a rabbi. In the intuitive stream drawing, I saw a spade and what looked like a person with a yarmulke on. I really didn't know what a spade meant for me and kept pondering it. When the rabbi and I spoke, I told her I had meditated and that a spade image emerged. She said, "Well, I just now returned from a funeral, and we all held the spade one by one as we said goodbye, placing dirt into the ground." I was very glad I shared the spade image with her because it felt so synchronistic (and a little sad because of the funeral). I enjoyed the literal meaning; it was powerful for me even though I had initially been unsure of what a spade symbolized. Now I do have a strong association for spade (saying good-bye and religious ritual, perhaps); I will keep those associations in mind in case I see one again.

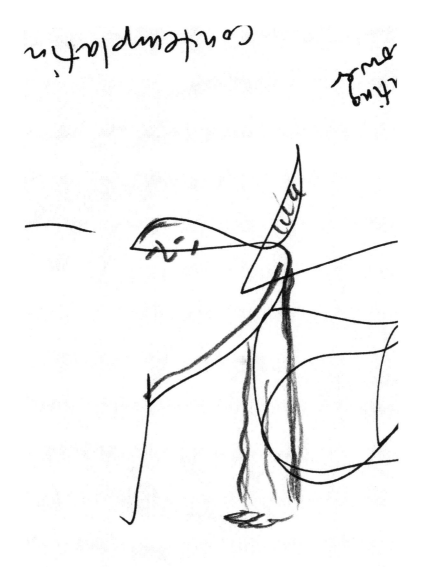

Wise Spirit Guide

I saw an old man in this intuitive stream drawing reading, his head low, holding a walking stick. He was moving to the left on the page (left direction meaning "the past" for me, right would be "the future"). I felt this meant perhaps the client had a significant past connection with wisdom from an elder who taught her, or that she was still learning from the past in a meaningful way, intentionally focused on becoming wiser. When I described the image and its meanings for me, she gleefully told me that she meditates and often sees an old man with a cane in her mind's eye, whom she believes is a guide to her. So it felt like a sign to her from one she considers her spirit guide! What would a man with a walking stick convey to you? Do you think of someone like Ghandi, perhaps, or do you get any other thought or feeling associated with such an image?

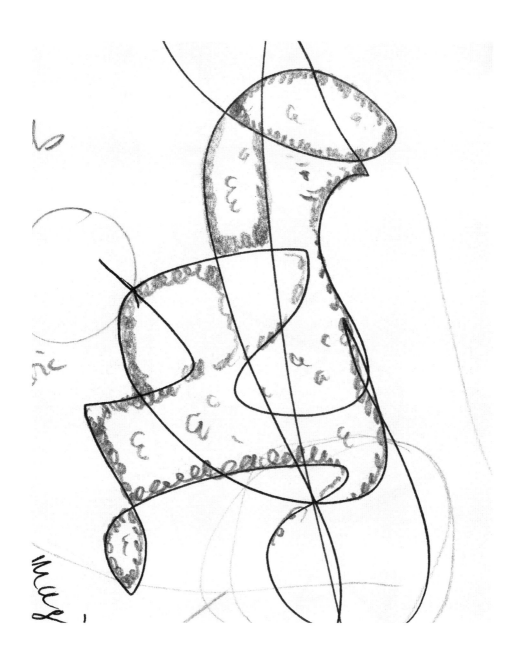

Loyalty and Companionship

What would you do if you saw a poodle in your intuitive stream drawing? For me, I felt love and happy companionship when I saw this image in a recent drawing. "Dog" for me represents trust, loyalty, and unconditional love. It makes me ask, "Who do I trust? Who deserves my trust? Am I trustworthy?" (After sharing the poodle image, the client confirmed for me with real surprise that she in fact owns a poodle she very much loves! The poodle helps keep her spirits up, gives her joy, and keeps her young.)

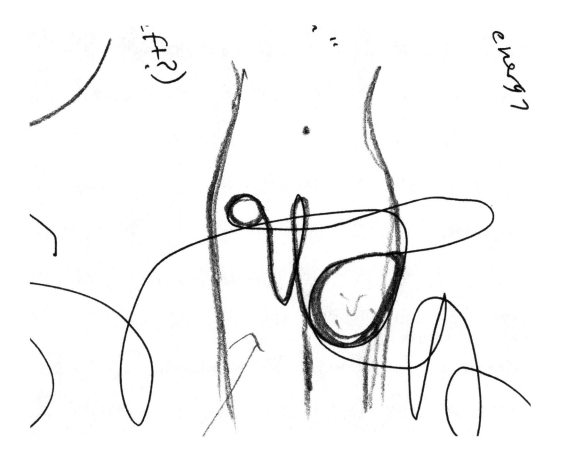

Primal Root: Ovaries

Can you see why I saw in this chakra chart image an area that reminded me of female reproductive organs? In my meditation, when I found the image by gazing it appeared asymmetrical, and there was one ovary that looked large and heavy. I thought it was worth exploring but didn't want to alarm the client. I just described it and asked the client if she had any water-weight gain or pain or anything relating to the image. She said she had had one ovary removed, so the image made sense in a literal way, and we moved on to other points of discussion. For me, and for her, it affirmed an experience she had, but it did not necessarily need to have a deeper meaning.

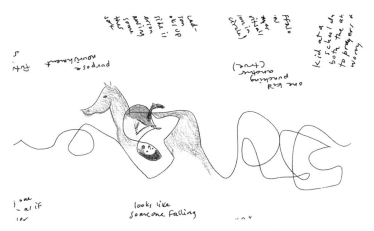

Figure 20b. My stream drawing of a person falling off a horse.

Figure 30. An image of sharp broken glass in an intuitive stream drawing reading.

Figure 31. An image of a car crash in an intuitive stream drawing reading.

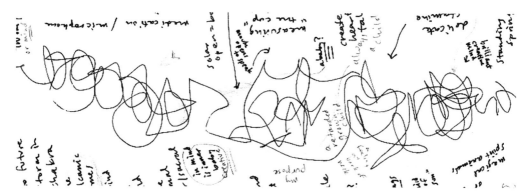

Figure 22. First time line.

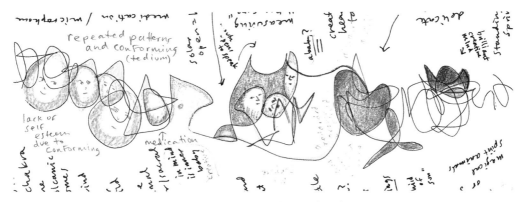

Figure 23. First time line, colored in.

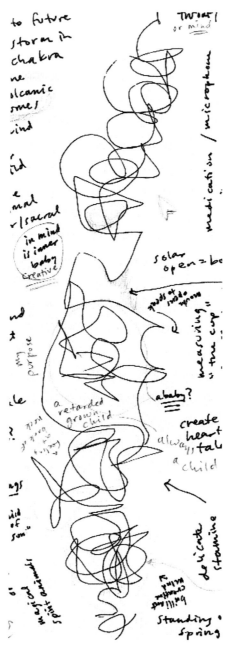

Figure 24. First chakra chart.

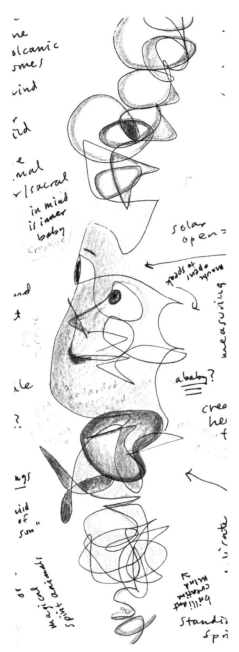

Figure 25. First chakra chart, colored in.

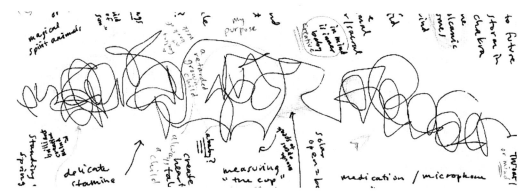

Figure 26. Second time line.

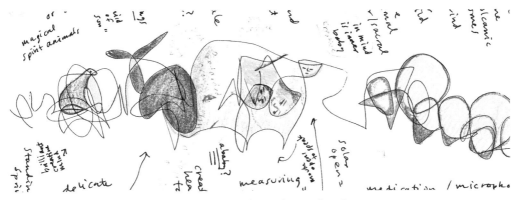

Figure 27. Second time line, colored in.

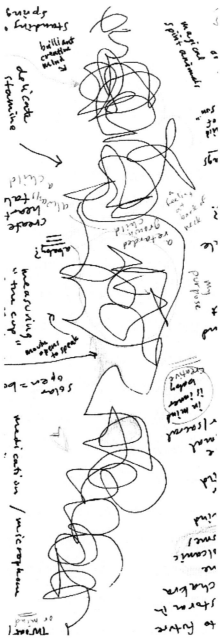

Figure 28. Second chakra chart.

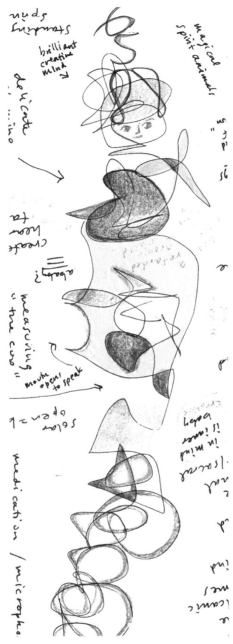

Figure 29. Second chakra chart, colored in.

Figure 32. Case Study: Love and Grief—Grandmother.

Figure 33. Case Study: Love and Grief—Grandmother, colored in.

Figure 34. Case Study: Love and Grief—Attacker.

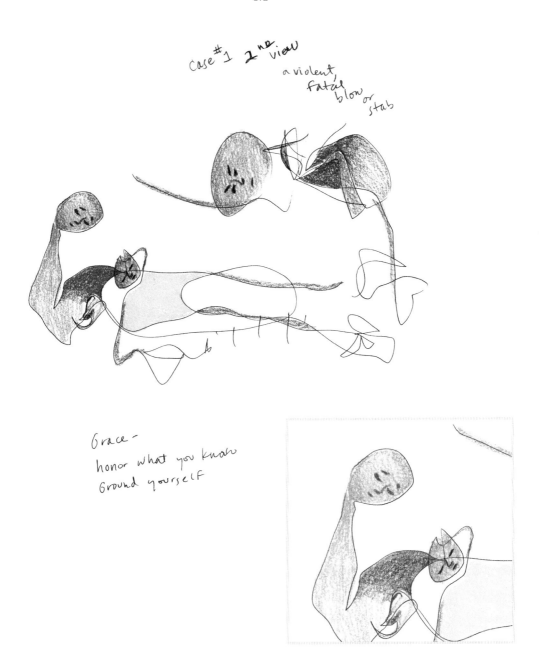

Top left, Figure 35. Case Study: Love and Grief—Attacker, colored in.
Lower right, Figure 36. Case Study: Love and Grief—Attacker, detail (witness to the attack).

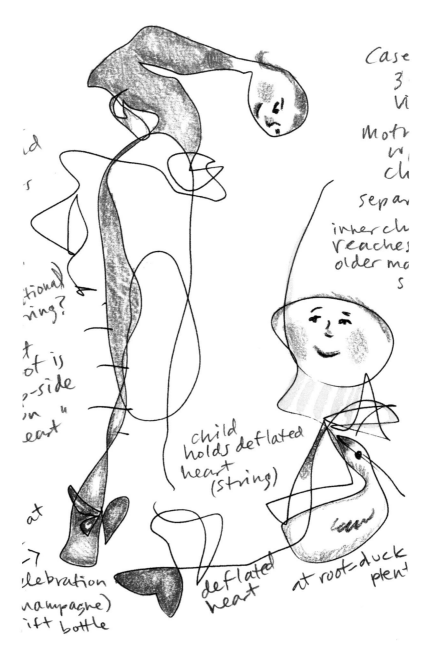

Case
3
v...

Mot...
v...
ch...

sep...

inner ch...
reaches
older m...
s...

id

s

tional
ing?

t is
ot is
-side
in "
eart

child
holds deflated
heart
(string)

at

->
lebration
nampagne)
ift bottle

deflated
heart

at root=duck
plen...

Figure 37. Case Study: Love and Grief—chakra chart, detail (apron strings).

Figure 38. Case Study: Love and Grief—chakra chart, detail (child).

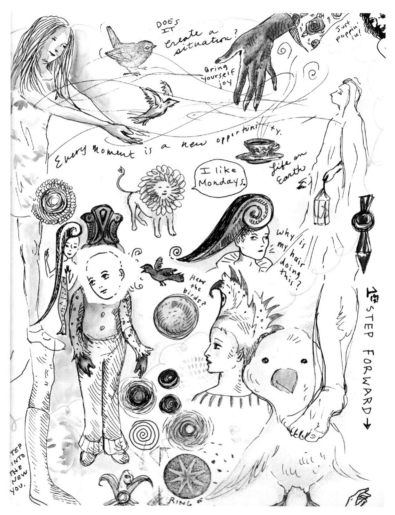

Figure 39. Little Streamers: sample in color.